# Bringing the Invisible into the Light

*spirituality*
*15/23*

## Some Quaker Feminists
## speak of their experience

## by the
## Quaker Women's Group

QUAKER HOME SERVICE · LONDON

First published August 1986
this edition August 1995
by QUAKER HOME SERVICE

ISBN  0 85245 199 7

Printed in Great Britain by Ipswich Book Co. Ltd., Ipswich, Suffolk.

# Acknowledgements

The task of compiling a book whose contributors and editors are widely scattered across Britain has posed logistical and financial problems not normally encountered by the individual author/illustrator and her editor. It has been necessary for us, as a group, not only to co-ordinate times and places for our meetings, but also to travel many hundreds of miles to participate in these gatherings. Our overall expenditure on both correspondence and travel has therefore been considerable.

Because financial independence is as rare among Quaker women as it is among women outside the Society of Friends, the publication of this book would not have been possible without the heart-warming support which we have received. We are glad to acknowledge the assistance given to us by several Quaker Trusts, Monthly and Preparative Meetings and individual Friends.

We wish to thank the staff at Charney Manor for the warmth of their welcome whenever we worked at The Gilletts.

We have valued the encouragement given to, and the faith shown in us by Elisabeth Salisbury and Janet Scott, our Swarthmore Lecture Committee contacts, and we are grateful to Clifford Barnard for his co-operation and help over technical matters.

To all these, and to others unknown to us who supported individual women, our grateful thanks.

# *Domesticity*

If I lay down my pen to wash their dishes,
How shall the world read what I have not written?
Others may write, but none convey my vision:
And we shall forever eat frugally off clean plates.

# Contents

# Introduction

Writing this Swarthmore Lecture as a group has been a unique experience. From the beginning, we were clear that we wanted this to be a co-operative endeavour involving us all. The form of that involvement has varied according to each woman's interest and abilities, and the time and energy she has been able to give.

This process, as important as the product, has been both stimulating and frustrating. It has involved pain and tears, fun and laughter. We have met together in small groups, in each other's homes and at The Gilletts, Charney Manor; we have trusted one another with some of our deepest experiences. Not least has been the sharing of our written words, distilled through the group's editing into this present volume. For us, this book is a beginning, a first saying of things that we have thought and known and experienced, but not before acknowledged publicly. We have brought the invisible into the light.

In some of these pieces there is great pain, yet underpinning many of them is a message of hope – the knowledge that, although this is how things have been, already they are changing, we are changing. *Bringing the Invisible into the Light* affirms our process, allows others to see it too. We hope that Friends will read our words with open eyes and open minds. We have a vision of the future, when everyone shall be free to reach their full potential. Is not this the essence of true religion?

Quaker Women's Group

# - *Interweaving Quakerism and Feminism*

*'Take the common things of life and walk truly among them'[1]*

Both Quakerism and Feminism are part of the fabric of my life. To me they offer visions which overlap – and each enlarges the other. Reading, thinking and, above all, talking about the insights which Feminism offers is a vital part of my spiritual journey. When I find these insights reflected in the history and practices of Friends, I feel immensely supported on that journey. (In fact, although I had come to meeting for worship on odd occasions over several years, it was finding Feminism in the Society in the shape of the Quaker Women's Group that changed me from a very tentative enquirer into a member.)

In talking with Friends, I do not find that the links between Feminism and Quakerism have been sufficiently valued – or, indeed, their relevance to women today acknowledged. The connection has more often been documented in Feminist 'herstory' than in Quaker 'history'. But it has been a continuing joy to me to discover the long association of Quakers with Feminism (as well as Quaker enterprises with a Feminist flavour). The English Quakers Margaret Tanner, Mary Carpenter and Mary Priestman were influential in persuading Josephine Butler to take up her campaign for the repeal of the notoriously anti-woman Contagious Diseases Acts; Josephine Butler herself reckoned Quakers first among the religious groups supporting the campaign. It was a Quaker

1

Feminist, Anne Knight, who was the first to produce a written publication advocating women's suffrage in Britain and the first to bring a petition on this subject before the House of Lords. The support of New York Quakers for Elizabeth Blackwell, the first woman to succeed in being recorded as a doctor on the British Medical Register, was critical in enabling her to establish her practice.

The intertwining of Quakerism and Feminism can be seen most clearly in the life of Lucretia Mott. I do not know whether the relative ignorance about her among English Quakers owes more to English insularity or to the general tendency of a male-dominated culture to excise women from the record. In either case it is a sad loss. She was a valiant figure and an inspiration to any Quaker with Feminist leanings or any Feminist with Quaker leanings. Prominent in the anti-slavery movement in America, she was sent as a delegate to the 1840 Anti-Slavery Convention in London. Along with other American women delegates she was not allowed to take part because of her sex. The women were forced to sit behind a screen and it was here that she met Elizabeth Cady Stanton, who later proclaimed this meeting the beginning of her real Feminism. The association of the two women later bore fruit in the Seneca Falls Convention, one of the key events in generating the powerful 19th century movement for women's suffrage in the United States. It is instructive for us to note that of the five women most central to the organisation of this conference, four (Lucretia Mott herself, her sister Martha Wright, Mary Ann McClintock and Jane Hunt) were Quakers and that of the signatories to the radical Declaration of Sentiments that it issued the largest single religious group represented were also Quakers.

The strands of Quakerism and Feminism weave together in their joint sense of a 'wholeness of Spirit' – their connectedness to the wider world. Friends have a tradition of involvement in social and political activity springing from the recognition of 'that of God in every one'; the understanding that true peace is impossible without justice has led many individual Friends to be concerned with different facets of our community life. Anne Downer's concern for the poor, Lucretia Mott's for the rights of blacks, slaves and women, and Elizabeth Fry's for prisoners have all resulted in continuing Quaker activity in these spheres.

As Feminists we find ourselves in a similar situation. Once we have understood the mechanisms that work against us as women, we cannot close our eyes to the ways in which they work against other groups and against us all working together for our common empowerment. We draw together in groups such as Women for Life On Earth, which sets out to 'promote the links between peace, ecology and feminism'.

But this shared acknowledgement of 'connectedness' springs from a deeper unity between the two movements. This unity is to be found in two principles which, though perhaps differently expressed, yet underly the practice of both: the call to trust our own deepest experiences and to share out equally with others the responsibility for our communal life.

*'And this I knew experimentally'*[2]

The first of these, the call to trust our own deepest experiences, is accurately summed up for Quakers in one of George Fox's questions which led to Margaret Fell's convincement, 'You will say, Christ saith this, and the apostles say this; but what canst thou say?'[3]

This question challenges us to reconsider the interpretations others offer us: not to take on trust what we have read or understood at second hand, but to test it against our own experience. We must base our lives on the leadings of the Inner Light as it comes to us.

The question has a particular poignancy for Feminists. It is one of the central insights of Feminism that the accepted

3

wisdom, the public reality, is at best partial, reflecting over-whelmingly the experience of being male in our culture. So the experience of understanding that we not only can, but *must*, set that aside and answer from our own lives, is truly liberating.

The language in which we express what we find we *can* say is of vital importance: it both shapes and reflects our values. One result of the emphasis on Plain Speech by early Friends was to challenge the class hierarchy of the day. The emphasis on non-sexist language by present-day Feminists is likewise a challenge to hierarchy, in this case the sex hierarchy, which women have brought into the Light by naming it — patriarchy. The challenge is recognised, though not of course acknowledged, and this is why non-sexist usage is resisted and its significance denied. Our Quaker tradition enables us to recognise that our choice of language, and our reaction to the choice that others make, reveals values which may other-wise stay hidden.

But George Fox's searching question has another challeng-ing aspect. It is not enough to test our understanding inwardly and privately. We must *say* what we find. As Quakers we can all testify to the central place that our Meet-ing has in our lives. We share our dim apprehensions of the Light and test our concerns against the wisdom and percep-tions of the rest of our Quaker community. As Friends we 'seek to know one another in the things which are eternal'. As Friends too we seem to feel a need to gather together in groups to share concerns about our social and working lives, in the fields of education, medicine, the arts and so on.

The experience of countless women in the Consciousness Raising groups which are a key feature of the contemporary women's movement is very similar. We feel a need to gather together to talk about our lives in all sorts of areas and we can testify to the power that comes from sharing: we have dis-covered that our connectedness goes deeper. We are not alone in our experiences of exclusion; other women have shared our pain and this has made us Sisters. We are Sisters because we share meanings forged in the fire of personal experience, however much they may be at variance with the accepted wisdom. As Sisters we have a commitment to those meanings. In the words of Elizabeth Cady Stanton, who worked so tirelessly for women's suffrage,

> 'Through suffering we have learned the 'open sesame' to the hearts of each other. There is a language of universal significance . . . by which with a sigh or a tear, a gesture . . . we know the experiences of each other in the varied forms of slavery.'[4]

### *'In the light, everyone should have something to offer'*[5]

Holding that truth is to be discovered by each person testing their own experience, both Quakers and Feminists recognise that each must be heard and their experience attended to. As Quakers we are accustomed to the formula 'that of God in every one' and to meetings for worship which are made open to all comers so that fresh Light can enter. We require no declaration of faith beyond that implicit in coming to Meeting. Most Feminist groups operate in the same open way: there is no requirement to agree to any statement of policy before you can participate, merely an agreement that the work of the group is valuable.

In both Quaker groups and Feminist groups, I have been glad of this acceptance of the value of the individual contribution. I have been struck by the way in which visions, opinions and styles of expression that I have rejected at the time they were put forward have later seemed to be of the very essence of the matter. Ministry in Meeting on animal rights that I once thought trivial now seems to me to point clearly to the way in which we exploit the environment in which we 'live and move and have our being'. Sisters asserting that it is male violence that lies at the root of the disease in our culture once seemed to me to be extreme but now seem quite prophetic.

Since all are equal participants in the group, all must share the responsibility for decisions. How much sweat has been expended to give this insight practical form! Through the changing experiences of its 300 years, the Society of Friends has by and large opted for formality with defined roles and structured groups of Meetings. At some points this has allowed elders a disproportionate amount of power and influence and when Women's and Men's Meeting were separate, they did *not* have equal status. Feminists have moved from more traditional structures towards informality with a distrust of hierarchy in any form and the use of loose networks. Sometimes this has led to a lack of coherence and clarity. Quakers and Feminists have much to learn from each other in this area.

However, despite their divergent paths, Quakers and Feminists have both recognised that 'there is a better way of doing things'[6]. They both share an understanding that the right decision can only be reached by a process that allows everyone to unite behind it, an acceptance of the need for some form of consensus and a concern to share roles of responsibility.

### *'Stand still in the light'*[7]

Sharing so much else, Feminism and Quakerism inevitably share some problems. The openness, the lack of dogma, produces a group with many divergent views. The result can all too easily be fragmentation or, even worse, factionalism. The Society of Friends is currently experiencing an upsurge of so-called 'fringe groups', which are seen by some to threaten its unity and stability. Among Feminists also there are differences of emphasis: working with men versus working on our own, legislative action for equal rights versus positive discrimination for women, revaluing of women's traditional contributions to society versus child-care facilities to enable them to take up wider roles – and so on. In any particular group or Meeting, these divergences may lead to a 'hidden conformity'. Thus if you apply for membership of the Society you may find your appointed visitors anxious to clarify whether you feel that you can describe yourself as a Christian and what Christianity means to you. In a roughly similar way, in some women's groups the group's understanding of Feminism may make it difficult for particular women to be full participants.

Both Quakerism and Feminism have a problem of commitment. Many Quaker Meetings have an ever-growing percentage of attenders, some of long-standing . . . and how many times have you heard the disclaimer 'I'm not a Feminist but . . .' preceding some comment well within the bounds of Feminism? It seems to me that this problem is in part a product of the divergence of views within both Quakerism and Feminism. People who are happy to associate themselves with some aspects of each of the movements do not want to be connected with other views which they see as either 'extreme' or 'limited'. It took me a long time to feel in my bones what I had understood well enough in my head: that I was 'my' sort of Feminist. I can speak for myself without feeling any need to disown my Sisters who may be coming from a different place and may be on a different journey: we will walk together as far as we can. Similarly, although I had felt part of my local Meeting for some time, it was only recently that I felt strong enough to be 'my' sort of Quaker and so apply for membership.

Quaker and Feminist groups both attract people who are trying to base their lives on a vision which society at large does not share. A majority of Quakers now join by convincement and many have experienced the confusion of finding that a familiar intellectual and emotional framework will

7

no longer serve and the pain of leaving a loved and valued Christian community elsewhere. In a male-dominated culture, there is a sense in which all women come to Feminism by convincement since, in doing so, they reject that culture's meanings. For most of us, there is the pain of recognising that the ways in which we have thought about our lives no longer hold true and that loved and valued relationships will have to change. To the extent that we are struggling with commitment to visions different from those around us we are all, in Quaker parlance, 'under concern'. As Quakers, we have long recognised that such people are not easy to live with. We experience difficulty in moving together and in harnessing our individual strengths to our collective aims.

### 'Dear Friends and Sisters all up and be doing'

Finally I have to say that from time to time in my experience of both Quakers and Feminists there has appeared a certain arrogance. Pondering on this arrogance in myself, I find it to be the reverse side of the coin of convincement. In discovering both Quakerism and Feminism, I have a strong sensation of not being able to go back. The Light has entered and there is no possibility of closing my eyes again. The convincement, and the pain that accompanies it as surely as the Light, signals a moving out on to unknown waters. The waters may be unknown to us, but are not uncharted, for many have travelled this way before. Our Quaker and Feminist forebears have left us the records of their journeys. Records are valuable to those whose deepest experiences contradict the accepted wisdom, and writing is a help in wrestling with the conflicts inherent in being 'peculiar people'. We must follow them in our common search for wholeness. In the words of the Epistle from the Women's Yearly Meeting held at York in 1698, 'And therefore dear Friends and Sisters, all up, and be doing, and put your hands to the work and your shoulders to the burden . . .'

# Bringing the Invisible into the Light

'Bringing the Invisible into the Light' evokes a sense of a constant search for truth, a struggle to overcome complacency and a striving to bring all aspects of life under the ordering of the Spirit. Light illuminates the darkness, enables one to see further, to see that which had been hidden. Often it is with reluctance that we allow ourselves to look into the darkness, to drag out prejudices and allow ourselves to change, to be transformed. Our eyes *are* reluctant to see and our ears fail to hear.

When John Woolman brought his recognition of the evil of slavery to Quaker Meetings, he met with resistance. Since he personally refused to wear the products of slave labour, he cut a strangely garbed figure whose very appearance was a reminder of the whole issue. He travelled under concern, asking Friends to look at their ownership of slaves and whether this sat easily on their consciences. This was no academic exercise but a challenge on the personal level. The awkward, discomforted feelings, the rush to find excuses, are almost tangible to us even after all these years.

Lucretia Mott, the Quaker Minister, also made many uncomfortable, in making the connections between the position of women and that of slaves:

'Too long have wrongs and oppressions existed without an acknowledged wrongdoer and oppressor. It was not until

9

the slave holder was told 'Thou art the man' that a healthy agitation was brought about. Woman is told that the fault is herself, in too willingly submitting to her inferior condition, but like the slave, she is pressed down by laws in the making of which she had no voice, and crushed by customs which have grown out of such laws. She cannot rise therefore, while thus trampled in the dust. The oppressor does not see himself in that light until the oppressed cry for deliverance.'[8]

We have heard the challenge of John Woolman. Have we also heard the challenge of Lucretia Mott? Look at the position women occupy in society today. Is it a just one? Do the institutions and laws still need changing to rectify a wrong every bit as evil as slavery? This challenge is still relevant today.

# Women and the Society of Friends

One of the ways in which I came to the Society of Friends was through a growing knowledge of its history. My religious experience, from a very young age, has been informed by a historical sense and I believe that,

'Time present and time past
Are both perhaps present in time future
And time future contained in time past.'[9]

As I have become increasingly involved in the Quaker Women's Group, I have taken a special interest in the history of women in the Society of Friends – Quaker herstory. This has lead me to two lines of enquiry which might profitably be followed.

The first is the recovery of the lives of Quaker women of the past. They are so often found only obliquely in the public record, reflected in the lives of fathers, brothers and husbands. My second line of enquiry is into the position of women in the Society of Friends and in particular the history of separate women's meetings.

There are several themes that can be discerned in the history of women and Quakerism, which may be briefly set out as follows:

That George Fox had an ideal of complete equality between men and women, but that he recognised that to achieve it

11

would require effort on both sides. It was to this end that he set up separate women's meetings.

That, from the later years of the 17th century and particularly after Fox's death in 1691, this ideal became diluted by a growing conservatism and that in order to preserve the authority of men over women, a split was made between spiritual and temporal matters, contrary to the original spirit of Quakerism. Equality was accorded to women in the spiritual sphere, so that men's authority in the temporal sphere, including the running of the Society, might not be disturbed.

That even spiritual equality was in practice dependent on women remaining within their so-called 'natural' sphere of influence, and not encroaching upon the more serious concerns of men.

That through it all, it was the women's meetings, however little outward power and influence they possessed, that helped women to keep the ideal of full equality alive. They have passed it from generation to generation and even today, when it appears that equality can be taken for granted, there is a need for this tradition to continue.

George Fox believed in the equality of men and women and that, 'if the power of God and the Seed spoke in man or woman it was Christ'[10]. His original vision was that as Christ had 'come to teach his people himself',[11] then the Second Coming had already taken place, and social relationships occasioned by the Fall, including the authority of men over women, were no longer relevant. Fox's ideal was that men and women should work together as 'helpsmeet' and 'co-heirs' in the new Gospel Order. Not surprisingly, women found this vision particularly attractive and from the early days of the movement took a full part in preaching and organisation.

In London, around 1656, two important women's meetings were set up. The Women's Two Weeks Meeting was begun at the instigation of the Men's Two Weeks Meeting, and was funded by them. The reason for its setting up was later recounted by Edward Burrough as follows, 'It was seen and considered by us that the affairs concerning Truth being grown more large daily, and that it was not so proper for the Men as for the Women to visit the sick and to search out the necessities of the poor, weak, widows and aged, that therefore the Women Friends should keep a like Meeting . . . to be assisting in what was convenient to the Men . . . and that provision should be made for them . . .'[12].

At the same time another similar meeting was set up at the instigation of the women themselves. As George Fox tells it, 'I came to Gerrard Roberts' house about eight in the morning and there came in Sarah Blackbury to complain to me of the poor . . . So I spoke to her, to bid about sixty women to meet me about the first hour in the afternoon . . . And what the Lord had opened unto me I declared unto them concerning their having a meeting once a week, every second-day that they might see and enquire into the necessity of all Friends who was sick and weak and who was in wants, or widows or fatherless in the city and suburbs . . .'[13]. This came to be known as the Box Meeting after the box into which each member put her contribution as she came into the meeting.

These two meetings had approximately the same personnel and were referred to jointly as the Women's Meetings of London. They thrived and showed that women were quite capable of running business meetings themselves, including keeping the accounts.

From the 1670s onwards, George Fox was much concerned with setting up a network of meetings for business and discipline as well as worship throughout the country. The setting up of women's meetings was a constituent part of this organisation. Fox saw the value of separate women's meetings as two-fold. Firstly, if women met together they might grow in confidence and ability so as to take their full place in the Gospel Order in a way which would be impossible if they always met with the men. Secondly, Fox was concerned to give women separate responsibility for what he saw as their 'natural' sphere of activity. This was to care for the poor, the sick and prisoners, to take charge of the welfare of children and young people, particularly young women, and to investigate and approve proposed marriages.

Even such limited aims provoked a storm of opposition and allowed deep-seated, traditionally male attitudes to surface. The question was the old one of authority. It was acceptable for women to busy themselves with the poor, that was their proper sphere, but to be able to overrule a proposed marriage gave them too much power.

Not all men were ready to be helpsmeet. Nathaniel Coleman made his position clear when he asked Fox 'whether it was not the command of God that a man must rule over his wife, and he would rule over his wife'[14]. Thomas Curtis of Reading, refusing to allow the Women's Quarterly Meeting to use the Meeting House, stated that it was not suitable that women should go gadding about the country, away from their household duties.

The women's meetings held together strongly in spite of opposition, or perhaps because of it. As Mary Elson, one of the mainstays of the London meetings, said, 'blessed be the name of the Lord who hath quickened and made alive unto himself and hath knit and tyed and bundled up and hath united us together in one Spirit.'[15]

However, the fear of women's usurpation of men's authority had been expressed and made itself more evident as the first revolutionary enthusiasm faded and a more traditional, respectable spirit pervaded the Society. No-one denied the spiritual equality of men and women, but a distinction came to be made between spiritual and temporal. As William Loddington put it, 'So Male and Female are all one in Christ, that is in Spirituals, but Man the Head in Temporals.'[16]

*". . . hath knit and tyed and bundled up . . ."*

This sort of thinking particularly affected those business meetings whose membership included both men and women. For example, Six Weeks Meeting, concerned with property and financial matters in London, was originally constituted by Fox of about equal numbers of both sexes. However, a perusal of the minute books suggests that this equality was increasingly more apparent than actual. Even from the start the men attending were always listed first, and as time passed and the first generation of members disappeared, the number of women actually attending became very small. There were often only one or two and from about 1728 only men attended. I have yet to ascertain when the formal membership of women was discontinued, but it had certainly happened before the 19th century.

As the forces of conservatism grew stronger, even women's spiritual equality was sometimes compromised. The ministry of men came to be seen as paramount and by 1701 we find Morning Meeting suppressing an incipient meeting of women ministers with the words, 'This meeting finding that it is a hurt to Truth for women Friends to take up too much time, as some do, in our public meetings, when several public and serviceable men Friends are present and are by them prevented in their serving, it's therefore advised that the women Friends should be tenderly cautioned against taking up too much time in our mixed public meetings.'

The distinction between spiritual and temporal authority and the difficulties that arose from this are particularly well illustrated by the history of the Women's Yearly Meeting.

From the earliest days of the Society there had been a meeting of women Friends at the time of Yearly Meeting, both in London and York. It issued epistles, which were sometimes printed, for circulation in this country and abroad, but it was not a meeting of record and had no legislative power. The women felt limited in their ability to influence either their sisters or the Society at large and from at least 1746 there were attempts to achieve official status, but without success. The argument against, put forward in 1766, makes it clear that women in general were thought incapable of taking an equal part with men. 'The forming of such a Meeting hath appeared to our predecessors, as it doth to us, a matter of great difficulty. As therefore the meeting of a number of Women Friends and of suitable abilities to carry on so weighty and important a work appears to us as very doubtful and uncertain and can but subject the few who are qualified to assist in this work to great inconveniency, it is therefore our unanimous opinion that the present is not the proper season for complying with the proposal.'[17]

A Women's Yearly Meeting was finally set up in 1784, with the support of visiting American women, particularly Rebecca Jones of Philadelphia, but the point was not easily gained. One man remarked 'that it would be preposterous to have a body with two heads', an objection which shows his view of male authority, but Rebecca Jones gave an answer which stressed equality. 'There is but one Head to the body which is the Church, even Jesus Christ, and in Him male and female are one.'[18]

Even with this point gained there continued to be a good deal of conflict about women's meetings. Often private comments reflect the state of mind of the Society or at least of certain members of it, more faithfully than does the public record. I have only space for one example here. At Yearly Meeting 1793 Anna Price and Martha Routh were appointed by Women's Yearly Meeting to report on their proceedings to the men. Having done this Anna Price reports, 'We were followed out of meeting by a certain young man who was fearful we should be too much set up, and convey too much encouragement to Womens Meetings . . . painful is the jealousy of Men Friends.'[19]

Throughout the 19th century women's meetings continued to wield a largely indirect influence. The Women's Yearly

Meeting provided a valuable opportunity for women to meet together, to gain experience of large gatherings and to join in the writing of epistles, but it played no part in the running of the Society.

There was some communication between the two Yearly Meetings but the women were expected to keep their place. They might exhort the men, but were not expected to be controversial, even on spiritual matters. For example, in 1836 Sarah Grubb and Ann Jones addressed the Men's Yearly Meeting on the Beaconite controversy, over the relative authority of the Inner Light and Scripture. Reactions were mixed, but Luke Howard for one was so incensed at their temerity that he had to be physically restrained from interrupting.[20]

If women wanted to become involved in temporal concerns they had to channel their energies into other philanthropic associations, often outside the Society. However, as the century went on, outward issues such as temperance and the opium trade occasioned many visits between the men and the women and some joint sessions on particular topics were held. These became more frequent and gradually a need was felt for women to become more involved with the Society as a legislative body. Eventually, in 1896, women were made eligible to be members of Meeting for Sufferings. Some doubts were expressed about the practicality of such a step. As Thomas Pumphrey put it in a letter to Isaac Sharp, the Recording Clerk, 'The women's voices are heard only in a very small minority . . . If Woman Friends *would* give us their opinions in equal numbers with men, either the time occupied would be doubled, or the self-restraint would have to be two-fold on the part of the men'.[21]

However, once this step had been taken it was logical and inevitable that the Women's and Men's Yearly Meetings should be amalgamated. From 1897 most sessions of Yearly Meeting were open to both men and women, and the first wholly joint Yearly Meeting was held in 1908. The closing

Minute of Women's Yearly Meeting 1907 speaks of 'mingled feelings' and certainly some tried to retain a place for women to meet together by holding a women's conference at the time of Yearly Meeting, but this only continued until 1918. Throughout the country women's meetings survived longer, probably as long as the lives of their adherents. The last of which we have a record was in Westmorland in 1944.

From that time until the present there has been no official way for women Friends to meet together. Perhaps there has really been no need and we have indeed reached that goal of perfect equality that Fox envisaged. But perhaps in our relentless forward progress, this particular door ought not to have been shut so firmly behind us. As Margaret Hope Bacon says, 'it appears to many contemporary students that the separate women's meetings provided Quaker women with a support group which they have somehow lost in their progress towards equality.'[22]

Certainly I know from experience that Quaker women meeting together can still be of use in strengthening each other and in stirring one another up to take our full part in the life of the Society of Friends as well as society at large. We are encouraged to follow not only our traditional 'natural' paths, but whatever way seems right for us as individuals.

It will do no harm to examine the assumption that 'there has always been equality in the Society of Friends'. Complacency is dangerous and limits the possibility of growth. If we can understand the ways in which Fox's ideal of equality has been compromised in the past, we will be more able to strive towards it in the future. It may be painful to bring the invisible into the light in this way, but it is better to take proper pride in our real achievements than to shelter behind half-truths and wishful thinking. Above all I believe it is important not to forget the women of the past who have striven to keep the ideal alive. The women who met at York in 1688 still have something to say to us today when they exhort us to 'answer Truth... and these our Testimonies cast not carelessly into a corner, but sometimes peruse them, and mark well the wholsom advice therein, that our travail may be answered, the Lord honoured, and you reap the benefit...'[23].

# Re-cycled Genesis
## *There is that of God in every Woman*

In the beginning God created the heaven and the earth
And the earth was without form and void; and darkness was
upon the face of the waters.
And the spirit of God moved upon the face of the waters.
And God said: Let there be Light: and there was light.
And God saw the light that it was good; and God divided the
light from the darkness.
And God called the light Day and the darkness Night.
And Peace lay over all the land.

And there came men into the Peace
Claiming a likeness with God,
They were not that God, being not spiritual, but using the
same pronouns,
The Authority of Likeness shone through.

And the woman saw and behold! she was deceived and in
amazement she loved.
She loved a man in his Likeness to God.

In her beginning her parents created her form.
Potential and pliable was she without knowledge of herself
And her parents breathed upon her and made her in their
likeness

21

And as she grew she came to know the Authority of God-
likeness in her parents.
And it came to pass that when she saw the man, she loved, as
who would love her God, being deceived by the Likeness and
cautioned by their Authority.


But lo! the man was not that God and he did cause her travail
Until she saw his Un-likeness
When he did rise up against her
Shattering the ground of her being
Which she had founded on the Likeness.


Then in the silence and the chaos
Did she sit blinded by the pain
Of losing man-Likeness and parent-Likeness
Yea! Verily then did she call to her God in supplication for a
sign –
For authority to find a Likeness of her own in which to love
and have her being.


Gently, calmly, by little and by little she began to see again
the scattered fragments of herself and each was twinkling,
attracting her attention, with light from the original Peace
shining through.
Wondering she melted from the frozen unreality into Joy
As, glorying, she took each spiky fragment, recognising and
holding it into rounded wholeness,
Placing each reverently, side by side, by under, by round, by
through and over the others, she made her whole and it was
good.
Unknowing, uncaring for the time whether she would live to
be amazed and love again, she explored the coloured,
translucent beauty
Trusting in the glory of her creation.

# Bad Language

When I gently remonstrate with Friends about their use of 'man' to describe all human beings they are inclined to say that I am being over-sensitive and that I am failing to look at the meanings beneath the language. I do try to listen to 'the music behind the words', but the tune I hear offers me little comfort.

'Man' we are told is a generic term encompassing the whole human race. Yet, in such phrases as, 'Man is the only primate to commit rape'[24] or, 'Man's vital interests are life, food and access to females' or, 'his back aches, he ruptures easily, and his women have difficulty in giving birth'[25], we have clear evidence that 'man' here means the male of the species.

Recently a group of second-year sociology students were asked to collect pictures for a display *Man at Work*. What they did was to produce an interesting mural of men at work. They knew, or they had been taught, that 'man' includes female and male, yet when they were given a task to do they interpreted 'man' as male.

Hearing this I decided to try an experiment on my class of ten year olds in a Middle School. I asked them to draw four simple pictures of the following: children in the playground, teenagers on their way to school, people in the park, man at leisure. These children had all learned about Stone-Age Man and Bronze-Age Man; they had watched a television programme about man's conquest of nature, and listened for two terms to a BBC programme entitled *Man.* Had I questioned them carefully, they would have told me that 'man' meant men and women. In their pictures of children in the playground, teenagers on their way to school, people in the park, all thirty children had illustrated both sexes. For the fourth subject, man at leisure, twenty-eight pupils drew a picture of a man engaged in a leisure activity; golf, fishing, watching television. Only two pupils, girls who were sitting next to each other, drew a picture of a swimming pool, with children, women and men enjoying themselves. Some of my more sceptical colleagues tried the experiment with very similar results, even with the older children. Are the children at my school and the group of sociology students unrepresentative of humanity?

It is surprising, too, how often we 'think male' even when using apparently neutral terms. We frequently hear news items such as: 'Six people were taken to hospital, including three women' or, 'The Prime Minister entertained three Russians and their wives at Chequers this afternoon' or we may see notices stating, 'This concession is available only to lecturers and their wives and children'. People, Russians, lecturers, although sex-neutral terms, are seen here to have a male bias.

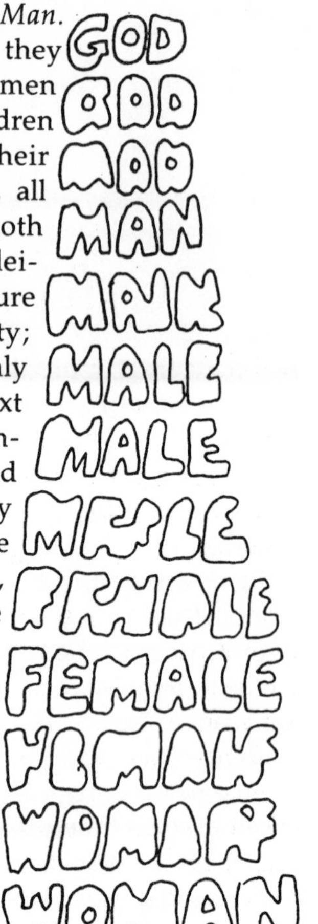

24

I believe that the way we use the English language is sexist and that it relegates women to a subordinate position. Feminists hold the view that society itself is constructed in a way which favours males. We can call this bias sexist, androcentric, masculist or patriarchal; it is located in our language itself. The social order under which we live is characterised by male dominance, and language is a means of perpetuating that dominance.

For instance, in linguistic studies, inventories have been compiled which show that there are far more words for males and that these are often of a more positive nature than those for females. At the same time it may be observed that many of the words for women carry sexual innuendos. Although there are altogether far more words for men, there are only twenty terms for a sexually promiscuous male, while for a sexually promiscuous female there are two hundred and twenty.[26]

There seems to be a close relationship between women's devaluation in language and their devaluation in society. Words, whatever their origin, become negative when they are used for women. This has been described as the semantic derogation of women.[27] Even when conditions are identical, such as that of bachelor and spinster, the female version is seen as pejorative. 'Old man' is a simple description, but 'old woman' can be used as a negative term. While titles for males retain their original positive meanings many female titles have undergone a downward slide, often ending up with a sexually debased meaning. Such examples are to be found in baronet and dame, courtesan and courtier, governess and governor, king and queen, madam and sir, and master and mistress.

The ordering of gender-related pairs of words such as the preceding is worth noting. Those given at the end of the last paragraph are in strict alphabetical order. So are the pairs: boys and girls, husbands and wives, man and woman. But are they placed in this order for that reason? It may seem petty to complain that the masculine is always placed first in such pairs, but it may seem less so when we look at the history of the custom. Since the sixteenth century, grammarians have insisted that the male gender is the more worthy gender and should, therefore, always be put first. In 1553 Thomas Wilson, a grammarian, complained very strongly about the word order of 'mother and father', claiming that to use the expression in this form was 'to put the cart before the horse', and pleaded, 'let us keep a natural order and set the man before the woman for manners sake.'[28] Are the compilers of our Books of Members in the Society of Friends honouring this 'grammatic rule' when they show such reluctance to use the more egalitarian alphabetical ordering of husbands' and wives' names? Why is it 'simpler and clearer' if we always put the man's name first?

Briefly I have tried to demonstrate a few of the many ways in which the English language is used to subordinate women and even render them invisible. We can, by using our language unambiguously, bring women more clearly into the picture. We can refuse to use the terms 'man' and 'he' except when these words refer specifically to the male gender. After all, it is not possible logically or mathematically to use the same words to describe the male gender exclusively and, at the same time, use it to include both men and women simultaneously.

I find it is often very painful to feel that I am excluded from some area that is central to my life or, perhaps even worse, to be uncertain about whether I am included or not. Our present language, devised and legitimated by male grammarians, often creates uncertainty and ambiguity for women. The English language is a living, flexible medium. With the changing nature of our society we must use our language to reflect and encourage that change. For women to become visible they must become linguistically visible. We must be ready to adopt new symbols, to recycle old ones, and to invest

our language with new images, if the male stronghold on
language is to be broken. We must be adventurous in con-
structing new forms, and in letting the old ones go. Let us
dedicate ourselves to bring the hidden, the uncertain, the
invisible into the light so that all human beings may be
accorded the dignity of language that is their right.

# The Names of God

God is our mother,
Father, brother,
Sister,
And any other
Name
That God chooses
To give us.

Compassionate, Merciful,
Loving and Just,
Source and Completion,
Beginning and End.

These are words
For the Word.

Forgive us,
For we know not
What they mean,
Unless we feel
Where words come from.

28

# 23

She is my guide so I need nothing more
She makes me lie down in green pastures
She leads me beside still waters
She restores my soul
She leads me in the paths of wholeness, the paths she creates.
Even though I'm scared of the dark, I know no fear
For she is with me
Her strength and her courage they comfort me.
She encourages me to approach those people I don't understand
And when she shows me her way
Then I do understand
I hope her example will be with me all the days of my life
And I shall dwell in her light forever.

# Encountering Eve

*Reflections on Genesis 3¹⁻⁶*

Now the serpent was more subtle than any other wild creature that the Lord God had made. He said to the woman, 'Did God say, You shall not eat of any tree of the garden?' And the woman said to the serpent, 'We may eat of the fruit of the trees of the garden; but God said, You shall not eat of the fruit of the tree which is in the midst of the garden, neither shall you touch it, lest you die.' But the serpent said to the woman, 'You will not die. For God knows that when you eat of it your eyes will be opened, and you will be like God, knowing good and evil.' So when the woman saw that the tree was good for food, and that it was a delight to the eyes, and that the tree was to be desired to make one wise, she took of its fruit and ate . . .

So familiar has this story become, so predictable its interpretation, we may dismiss it without a second thought. However, as we enter *experientially* into this strange encounter between Eve and the serpent, we may find that more is going on here than simply the seduction of a woman by some kind of evil principle.

Our understanding of these verses has become clouded by the way in which the serpent has been linked with evil. We are clearly told in the passage that the serpent is a creature of God, distinguished not by its evil intentions, but rather by its super-natural knowledge, its shrewdness and subtlety. The serpent does contradict God, but this does not necessarily mean that the serpent was opposed to God. On the contrary, I believe that the serpent was acting as a creature of God and was instrumental in drawing Eve into a new and vitally important awareness of, and relationship with, the creation.

Until Eve's encounter with the serpent, the humans had been curiously cardboard images who acted in a largely unseeing, unthinking manner. They give no indication that they recognise the goodness of the creation in which they find themselves. Nor do they thank God for it. After Eve's encounter with the serpent, however, she looks upon the tree, delights in it and desires its fruit. This is the first time any feelings are expressed by the humans in the creation narrative. As Eve looks at the tree, suddenly, we find a human being becoming conscious of creation, alive to it, moved by it and by the promise it offers.

I am not willing to blame Eve for eating the apple, neither am I willing to call it, unequivocally, a disobedient act. Eve recognised the tree as beautiful, and she wanted to partake of the fruit. She was additionally motivated by the dimmest thought that, somehow, through eating this fruit, she could also participate in divinity.

When we place ourselves, experientially, in the garden, we understand Eve in a fresh way. She was, I think, a person who imagined and gazed attentively. Through the periods spent brooding over the serpent and the tree, a thought had lodged itself in her mind: 'Perhaps things are not what they seem, perhaps this creation hides a secret, perhaps appearances are deceptive.' So, knowledge dawned on earth that there was more to this world than meets the eye. She had begun to see beneath the surface, and she found more than a serpent, more than an apple. Eve was out-growing the garden and the parent-God. She had embarked on a process of waiting, watching and wishful thinking; she had begun to wonder at the creation.

Now, wonder is a two-edged sword. We cannot experience wonder *at* creation, in the sense of being filled with awe, without also wondering *about* creation, in the sense of questioning. From the experience of wonder as awe, arises the possibility for thankfulness, for relationship, for pure devotion and for the deepest experience of God. From the experience of wonder as questioning, however, arises the possibility for anxiety and isolation. Our capacity to question confronts us with the truth that we are separate from the rest of creation. We know ourselves to be other than the natural world, in, but not completely of it.

Eve's wondering was awe-inspired and awe-inspiring. However, her wondering also inevitably caused her to question. It was this questioning which deprived her of her naïveté and set her for good or ill on a new path, which led away from the garden, away from the God of her childhood, and from the God of her dreaming innocence.

Eve must have eaten fruit in the garden before, but this fruit, this particular act was significantly different in intent. She was no longer eating out of a blind impulse to satisfy hunger; rather she was seeking to participate in the Wisdom of God. This was, in fact, a symbolic act of communion. It was an adventurous, even a dangerous act, but it was inspired by a hope which no one had ever dared hope before, that somehow, through the physical world, we might participate in spiritual reality.

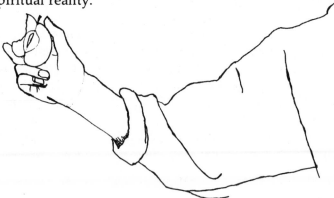

# Gospel Truth

In seeking to convey the meaning of their spiritual experience, women are moving towards a concept of God far removed from the old patriarchal image. In attempting to express the deepest fundamental truths about the reality of our existence we find that we need to use the personal pronoun 'I' – God in me – and 'I' am a woman. You might believe this to be a new, perhaps radical concept; but a major theme of Gnostic teaching is discovering the divine within and Gnostics perceived God as combining both masculine and feminine.

In 1945 thirteen papyrus books were found at Nag Hammadi in Upper Egypt. Although some were later lost or destroyed, there remain fifty-two texts from the christian era, including a collection of early christian gospels that were previously unknown. They had been buried for 1600 years, in all probability because of their suppression as banned documents.

Long before their burial, they had been declared heretical by the christian church. But who defined heresy, and for what reasons? The writers and users of these documents did not regard themselves as heretics, but as followers of Christ. In her book *The Gnostic Gospels*,[29] Elaine Pagels suggests that there were political as well as doctrinal reasons for choosing some books rather than others to form the canon of the New Testament. Pagels asks who made that selection, for what reasons, and why were so many other writings excluded, banned as heresy? Using the Nag Hammadi texts along with a range of other sources which have been known to orthodox tradition for over a thousand years, she offers a startlingly new perspective on the origins of christianity.

. The interest of the discovery for us is the light thrown onto a very different attitude towards both women and the feminine aspect of God. The absence of female symbolism for God is a mark of christianity.

'Theologians today are quick to point out that God is not to be considered in sexual terms at all, but the language they use daily in worship and prayer conveys a different message: God is *masculine*.'[30] The Gnostics continually use gender symbolism to describe God. Members of one group prayed to the divine Mother and Father. Valentinus suggests that the divine can be imagined as a dyad: in one part, the Ineffable, the Depth, the Primal Father; and in the other, Grace, Silence, the Womb and the Mother of all.[31] There are references to 'the Divine Mother the Holy Spirit' and to Wisdom, a feminine element. Some authors 'wondered to whom a single, masculine God had proposed, "Let *us* make man (Adam) in our image." ' Since the Genesis account goes on to say that humanity was created male and female, they concluded that the God in whose image we are made must also be masculine and feminine – both Father and Mother.[32] For the Gnostic, 'the divine is to be understood in terms of a harmonious, dynamic relationship of opposites – a concept that is akin to yin and yang but alien to christianity'.[33]

Even more interesting are the references in some books to women already known to us through the synoptic gospels. In the *Gospel of Philip* Mary Magdalene is described as Jesus' most intimate companion, the symbol of divine Wisdom. In *The Dialogue of the Saviour* she is spoken of as one of three disciples chosen to receive special teaching – praised above the other two: 'She spoke as a woman who knew the All.'[34]

34

New light is shed upon Peter – the rock upon which Christ built his church. The *Gospel of Mary* records a disagreement between Mary and Peter; in *Pistis Sophia* Peter complains that Mary is dominating the conversation with Jesus, and urges him to silence her; but Peter is rebuked. Later Mary tells Jesus, 'Peter makes me hesitate; I am afraid of him, because he hates the female race.' Jesus replies that whoever the Spirit inspires is divinely ordained to speak, whether man or woman.[35]

We are given clear evidence that women were highly regarded in gnostic circles: according to the Nag Hammadi texts, christianity showed a revolutionary attitude towards women. But from 200 A.D. we have no evidence of women in prophetic, priestly or episcopal roles. What might have been the effect on women, christianity and the whole history of western civilisation if gnostic ideas had been accepted as part of the rich fabric of our belief?

*Venus of Willendorf— oldest known figure of a person*

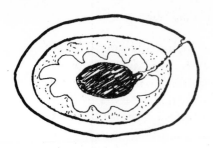

# The God of Our Fathers

When I was a little girl I was very much perplexed and pained by the idea of God as our Heavenly Father. What were the attributes of this God, the Lord God Almighty, this Majestic Father? Through my seven-year-old eyes God is authoritarian, stern, requires obeisance, loves me if I am good, has arbitrary powers (possibly terrifying ones) over my life, is punishing, knows everything about me, is everywhere and makes me into a supplicant, a dependant. If God loves me, as I was told, then it must have been from a great distance. This divine patriarch existed unto himself, Our Father. A dangerous and uncomfortable question always hung in my mind. What had he done with Our Mother? Why was she missing? It was a terrible slur and a source of secret pain that my mother who was powerful, loving and there (i.e. not distanced), had no divine counterpart.

It was no secret in our family that my father wanted a son and it grew in me that there must be something special, but hidden from me, about the relationship between father and son. The idea seemed significant. After all, God had a Son in whom He was well pleased. Could fathers have daughters in whom they were well pleased? Why didn't God have a Daughter? I do not smile now at this little girl who felt these things because it was a real loss, an exclusion from the scheme of things. Mothers and daughters had no divine counterpart; we were lesser. It also raised questions about my

36

relationship to my real father whom I loved and feared. Could I exist in a 'right' relationship with him if I wasn't a son? Could we ever really understand and accept each other or was the relationship inevitably and for ever flawed just because I was female? Alongside the feeling of not having a place in the divine scheme I learned as I grew up that to be female was to have attached to oneself many negatives. Women are perceived as emotional, irrational, weak, illogical, unreliable and talkative.

I learned of the dark side of being female – the blot of my sexuality. It was all a terrible muddle. We women are messy physically and emotionally. We bleed, we weep and being thus grounded in the physical and emotional, how can we be spiritual or rational? But worse than this; at puberty I learned that now I am become a woman I could have sex, conceive a child, I would now even have sexual feelings, but I mustn't own them. I had to stay untouched, clean, pure, wholesome, a girl, a virgin.

The Christian Church offers two very potent images for women which set the limits of our acceptability. We can be virginal: untouched by worldliness, innocent by virtue of asexuality and being pure in spirit, thus earn a place in the spiritual hierarchy. Or we can be motherly, nurturing, sacrificing. Safely past the messy business of childbirth we become the source of wholesome love, a sanctuary against the world, always there, giving our lives to the care of others. Virginal or motherly but not sexual. A sexual woman is a bad lot, a whore, a scarlet woman, dangerous. Women can take part in worship, receive the sacraments but like children we are not allowed to do things for ourselves. Whatever our experience of God, however deep our beliefs, however strongly we might feel we have a religious vocation, we cannot become priests.

I remember well at fifteen feeling a sullen resentment at my exclusion from the power of priesthood. I did not want to be a man, but I did want to take my place in the world fully. It seemed that being female meant not realising my potential.

Coming to Meeting was a liberating experience. In the discipline of silence I found the space to grow in understanding and I also felt that my experience of God or the divine was validated. In the absence of the authoritative male priest caste I began to gain the confidence that comes from shaping one's own meanings. I soon found that some ministry did not speak to my condition or that I could not yet understand it, but I learned something else very important. As a group of worshippers we often hear ministry which does not resonate in us but none the less we accept it as part of the life of the Meeting: accept it as an individual's offering which has *worth*. This acceptance of each other's worth was a relief and a release. I know that quite consciously in those early days of becoming a Quaker I put aside the whole knotty problem of God's maleness.

However, in the mid nineteen seventies the analysis feminists were making became 'mine'; I grew eyes and ears and I made connections. I could no longer deny what was happening in my marriage, my work-place, the messages in my head or body. It was a very, very painful process. To relinquish the fantasy of romantic love that I had been conditioned to expect as fulfilling; to acknowledge how deeply misogynist our society is; to see how grotesquely distorted are the values of a sexist culture, was almost unbearable. I didn't know how I could become strong enough to move on again.

In the midst of all this, having left the marriage, I found that I was pregnant. The powerful message that life goes on took me forward. In giving birth to my first child I had an experience which was to be the beginning of a different understanding of the ground of our spiritual being. I was pushing the baby out and suddenly the hot afternoon, the lonely little room, the white-clad midwives, the bored houseman, the pain, the consciousness of myself as an extremely tired woman in a most undignified posture, disappeared. I became completely centred in the act and I had a vivid inner vision of being at one with the cosmos; I felt very powerful. I felt I was taking part in the enormous act of creation.

The birth of my second child was attended by no such grace, but in the months following her birth I had a very frightening and enlarging feeling of having lost my individual identity. Instead I experienced myself as part of a long, long chain of mothers and daughters. For a while I did not know whether I was my mother, myself or my daughter. I became identified with all women. This loss of boundaries was very threatening. At the same time I knew it was very important to experience my connectedness to others at such a deep level.

In the labour and birth of our third child I discovered something else. I had this baby, at my insistence, at home, in the bed in which he had been conceived. On this occasion my loving partner, who had been a supportive but anxious presence at the birth of the second child, entered into a new relationship with me. Currently childbirth is seen as a medical event. I very much wanted this birth to take place at the pace I set, in my own environment. Here we were open to re-discovering that childbirth is a passion, a sexual passion. During this labour my partner held me, kissed and caressed me. I felt very cherished and loved. My sexual response speeded up and increased the intensity of the contractions. I experienced the pain as a powerful energy to ride forward on. It would not be untruthful to say that it was like a series of orgasms; certainly the power and intensity of feeling was orgasmic. Eventually of course, the midwife arrived so we had to forgo such intimacy.

The insights, that giving birth is a powerful creative act and can be a sexual passion, and that post-natal depression is a spiritual pointer, have implications for my understanding and evaluation of women's sexuality. Through these experiences of childbirth and the vital (living) tension of a deeply intimate, sexually passionate relationship, I have reclaimed *that* ground of my being as *spiritual*. This has put me in touch with that of God in me, and has important consequences for me in my spiritual quest. It has opened up my ideas about the nature of God. Women are part of the whole of creation and for me, if the idea of God is to have any meaning then it must include the whole of creation. It seems to me to be very important to name, recognise, value and revere that which is feminine in *all* our natures and in God.

For a long time now I have felt uncomfortable, sometimes pained, sometimes angry in Meeting to have God always referred to and imaged as male. I know that not all women recognise this as a disjunction or an exclusion but I would suggest that one of the reasons for this disclaiming is that the identification of the male as norm is so taken for granted, so unchallenged, that it is unconscious. It is also my experience that because Quakers do not have a male priesthood and because all men and women minister as they are moved, there exists the feeling that we have equality in the Society of Friends and do not have to worry about sexism.

My spirit knows that God is not male and my intellect and experience show me only too painfully the results of that way of talking about God. I suppose that at this point I have a question for Quakers. When are we going to take up the challenge of, 'in Christ there is neither male nor female' or of 'meeting that of God in everyone'? When are we going to acknowledge that the language we use to worship, pray and talk about God is deeply divisive and profoundly sexist?

# Letter to Joss

17th November, 1984.

My dear Joss,

I'd set this day, which was to have been your sixth birthday, aside, to lay my own ghosts, write my own memories and feelings, about you and about myself, down in some tangible way.

It has taken six years for the time to feel right for me to do so, helped to that moment by the love and support of friends who understand that I feel a need to do something, that there is unfinished business to attend to. When I first conceived this idea, of a day for myself, alone, to write or whatever felt right, it seemed simple. Somehow, I believed, the thoughts, facts and feelings of the past six years would spill out easily, neatly and chronologically onto a piece of paper. Not so. The past forty-eight hours have thrown all that into confusion and I realise that chronology has little to do with the jigsaw puzzle of events. What I had believed for all that time was over and gone is there, tangible and accessible.

After your birth, in those numb moments of shock, we gave willing and unregretted permission for a post-mortem. I remember offering your body to the hospital for research in the hope that maybe your death might not have been in vain. We elected not to have a funeral service for you – I felt that I could not bear seeing the grief that I had caused to others by failing to bear a normal, living child. Then I was helped by a

41

belief that the you that was you was perpetually around, and corporeal remains were irrelevant. I have since then, until this week, believed that at some time, unknown to me, your body was cremated. I remember, for a long time, watching for smoke from the crematorium chimney whenever I passed and wondering if it was you. Some dim memory told me that you hadn't been cremated alone, that your remains were in the coffin of someone else. I had a picture of you, after post mortem, like pieces of meat hastily shoved in at the feet of some other corpse and burned. I didn't dwell on it much, though I realise now that this is the picture I have lived with, quite clearly, all these years.

This week, knowing today was to be something special between the two of us, I almost unthinkingly rang the hospital. I don't know what I expected, nothing I think, after all long-ago cremated bodies are not something easily located; I think I wanted confirmation that there was nothing more to know and that that closed door could be locked forever.

Not so, that closed door is now wide open. I know now, beyond any doubt, what happened to you after we said our goodbyes so soon after your birth. You were buried, on November 23rd 1978, at 2.45 pm, in an unmarked public grave, in Southern Cemetery. For six years you have lain in the cold, wet earth, in a numbered grave which you share with six or seven others; some, babies like yourself who died before they'd lived, some who lived minutes, hours, or maybe days, and a few elderly people too.

The mixed emotions tear at me. Relief that my vision of so much meat, burned with someone else, and scattered to the four winds wasn't true. Anger that what I'd believed to be so wasn't true. Rage and pain that a body that should have been filled with warmth and life has been lying, unknown to me, in the freezing cold, rotting and decaying as if no one loved or cared. Guilt, rage and pain at myself for letting this happen. For failing to face up to the pain of that goodbye and knowing what had really happened; for shutting a door before it was ready to be closed. For acting as if I didn't care and as if it didn't matter. For failing to stand up strong, and take pride in my grief, failing to turn and face the pain squarely and honestly. For hoping that by ignoring it, it would eventually soften and dissipate. What I didn't know then is that that is never possible. Healing cannot come without pain, and without going deep into that pain the wound cannot heal with a clean scar. Instead there is only a healing over, leaving the pain to re-erupt at a later date.

You were buried, in a baby-coffin of your own, with no funeral service, but on consecrated ground. Today I went and found your grave, overgrown and covered in decaying leaves. I cleared it off and laid the last two roses from our garden there. Then I lit a candle for you and sat in silence for an hour or more. I wept, for you and those other babies all about you, for myself and my pain and grief. I felt anguish that you had been there for six years and I didn't know. My anguished desire was to tear up the stone to find and hold that precious body once more. Those seconds I held you for were not enough to build a lifetime of memories on. Then and now I wanted more. I wanted to tear at the earth to find that face and refresh the fading memory. To prove to myself that it all really did happen and wasn't some attention-seeking quirk of a diseased imagination. I've often felt the need for a public statement of your existence, a recognition that you were real. Maybe now I understand a little about the need for ritual, for that shared public statement, the need to share and acknowledge pain.

When you were born I remember panicking that you were going to be taken away from me without my ever seeing you. I recollect the urgency I felt, the strength of my need. I remember also being aware of an article I'd read about stillbirths, when I felt uncomprehending shock that people wanted to touch and see their dead babies and felt cheated when this was not allowed. My voice and what it was saying amazed me and the strength of my need was overwhelming.

They wrapped you up, like any other baby, and gave you to me. You were beautiful, you had red lips and your eyes were closed, sleeping so peacefully. Everything about you appeared perfect, normal and healthy. I kissed you goodbye and you were gone.

People were very kind. We went away to stay with friends and were accepted totally, shattered as we were. I kept going over what had happened, stressing to myself all the positive points: that your birth was a positive experience; that you hadn't been involved in the trauma of being born; that all you'd known was warm, watery darkness; that I couldn't feel guilty about what had happened, nothing could have been done or foreseen, so events could not have been otherwise; that something must have been wrong somewhere and that your death was somehow inevitable. But never once did I let in the pain, the fact that I hurt. I clung to how lucky I'd been and how much worse it could have been rather than feeling what was really there.

For me your death has become, over the past eighteen months, something improperly resolved; something that I've known that one day I must turn and face. Today has been the culmination of that need. I feel that much has been resolved, much doubt cleared away, the old wound finally cleansed. Hopefully now it can begin to heal clean and true. I feel satisfied with your birthday and justified in making it the way I did. I feel washed out and tired, but something feels at rest finally and I know now where you are. There are many more tears yet to be shed but it will, I believe, be a healing grief.

I love you and wish you peace.
Grant me forgiveness,

# Asleep Upstairs

They're asleep upstairs,
The young ones that define me

But theirs is the future
Theirs the need that confines me.

My future was their past—
Their definition undermines me.

Where is the help-meet
Who might give me alternative identity,
Who could rhyme with me?

No takers?

Am I bid nothing then
For parenthood?

All mine
This lonely, hallowed, respectable shrine?

Would that I were asleep upstairs.

# Slow Poison

I had a violent childhood.

I was born during the war, while my father was in the RAF. I could not recall my early childhood until a few years ago. Now an early memory of my father is of his holding a carving knife to my mother's throat as though he would kill her, telling me later that she 'deserved all she got and still had coming to her'. I was scarcely three years old.

Some two years later my father was demobbed. He brought me a beautiful present, a china doll with sleeping eyes, but held it back for a week while my mother made clothes for it. Wanting to make the giving of it something special, he put it on my bed; then in the middle of the afternoon he sent me to bed, ostensibly for naughtiness. I had not been naughty. I reasoned with him, but eventually had to give in. When I found the doll I was delighted. Almost at once anger took over, anger at the unnecessary hurt he had caused me. I rejected the doll, announcing scornfully that I wasn't going to play with it, ever.

I thought that was the end of the matter, but that night he raped me as a punishment for my ingratitude: the man's way of enforcing conformity on a recalcitrant woman – the soldier's way of dealing with an enemy. That this was about punishment was made clear in his parting admonition, '*Now*, go to sleep.' Lest my mother's anger should rebound on him, he threatened once more to kill her if she breathed a word. To protect me as well as herself, she didn't even mention it to me. How could I remember something that my own parents seemed to think had not happened?

It is not necessary that the victim consciously remember such brutality for it to be effective: I had only to be beaten for 'naughtiness' for all the terror, confusion and deep sense of my own wrongness to be evoked. I could not expect any help from outside the home, for what was happening within it was simply the attitudes of society practically expressed. At school I was frequently slapped on the hand and the boys were caned for very minor offences. Our friendly neighbourhood roadsweeper would chill our marrow with tales of how he daren't let his father know he'd been caned at school, for that would have earned him a further beating from his outraged parent. I had to live in my father's household until the age of seventeen. To do this I buried these painful memories, shut off my anger at these violations. I don't think he raped me again: he had no need to, for I was a cowed and timid child, needing no more than the threat of one of his thrashings to keep me in fearful obedience. He was always violent, and would beat me up on the slightest provocation. All the people who didn't want to know about it – teachers, shopkeepers, other children's mothers – chose to see it as punishment which I must have deserved. I had no option, it seemed, but to accept their view: so guilt kept me quiet.

While being taught christianity, at school and in church, everything I learnt reinforced the status quo: God was an Almighty Father, who didn't only catch you out sometimes when you hadn't covered your tracks, but who saw everything you did. He loved me, I was told, as my parents loved me – so at least I didn't have to struggle with a strange concept there. Forgiveness was a different matter. It seemed that God was somehow inconsistent, allowing us extra chances and paying us by results; incorrigibly bad people, like myself, got the wages of sin and the bonus of everlasting hell and damnation. Effort was never enough, only dramatic success could ever be rewarded, and even then you had to remember how lucky, and unworthy, you were.

I was able to avoid many hurts by sublimating a need to confront and understand what had been done to me by becoming 'religious'. To explain why such divine gifts as boyfriends, marriage and children were definitely out, I entered a convent. The convent was a strange mixture of experiences. My sexuality was totally denied, which felt safe, but at the same time I was constantly in trouble for being wrong – which was a feeling so closely tied to my sexuality that I could not distinguish one from the other. And I was constantly urged to submit myself to the will of the Father, while I prepared myself to become the Bride of Christ. Fortunately for my sanity, I was also expected to do Biblical Studies and Theology. I learnt how little choice the young girl Mary had had, given her Jewish upbringing – not to mention her Immaculate Conception. At the time, I identified her enormous courage in responding, 'Behold the handmaid of the Lord; be it unto me according to thy word.' I used her words every day to dedicate myself to that same Father-figure; only years later did I recognise the other similarities between her experience and mine.

At the same time, I was also learning how to respond to and develop my own spiritual awareness. After I left the convent, I was fortunate to find Friends. They gave me the permission, which I could not give myself, to reject the strait-jacket that christianity was for me. They also showed me, through the Peace Testimony and the technique of nonviolent direct action, that other ways than those I knew were possible.

I was still unable to make conscious all the connections to my father and his violence. I could see that this was at the root of my inability to find christianity meaningful; but the sexual violence remained occluded. In my (as I thought) new-found freedom from distress, I married a man so like my father that even to think of it is painful. The whole pattern of my childhood was repeated, with minor changes. There was no way that I could suppress the memory of all the thrashings and bashings that had been so frequent in my childhood, continuing throughout my adolescence, and no way that I would again tolerate physical violence. There was much verbal violence, and I cannot now distinguish much of our sexual encounters from that which, in other circumstances, I would call rape. Legally, rape in marriage does not exist, but when every quarrel must be settled by him penetrating me – even though I felt already hurt by him and totally unready for such a vulnerability – and when the only way I would be allowed to sleep was to yield to him, what else am I to call it but rape? But society perpetuates the myth of conjugal bliss, and effectively denies the reality of so much of our experience.

Next I had through feminism the experiences of so many other women with which to validate and interpret my own. I left my husband and renewed my spiritual quest. I learnt how to develop my own imagery, also how to develop the once so oppressive old imagery, in a way that would allow me to use its truth while retaining my integrity. I have developed a keen understanding of the ways in which society uses its primary institutions – the church, the school, and especially the family – to enforce and reinforce oppression. I have not recovered all the memories of my childhood and by that token I have yet to discover all the effects of violence on my life.

# Worth and Worship

I grew up in a very repressive, all-woman household. Children were to be seen and not heard (saying what we felt was 'answering back'), and were expected to obey our elders and betters without question. I did not know that males differed physically from females until I was nine or ten, when my grandmother's uncle repeatedly molested me. He told me I mustn't tell anyone, and indeed there is no way I could have. Eventually, to my great relief, my grandmother caught him in the act and made sure it never happened again. But the most damaging thing was that she quizzed me to find out to what extent I had been responsible. I know now that people often blame women for men's sexual actions, but at the time I got the message that my body (mySelf) was evil. I was dirty, fundamentally worthless, and guilty for what men did to me. The whole experience was as if I were falling through blackness, and the usual safety nets provided by family and society just weren't there. I kept on falling. As I became adolescent, I 'lost my faith in God', to use the terms of my evangelical upbringing.

For several years I completely repressed knowledge of the whole mess. I scrambled successfully for academic prizes which were a major source of self-esteem. Then after my daughter was born, madness and depression followed. The bottomless pit again. The turning point came when I realised that the root of it was my conviction that I was worthless. I decided that no-one could judge me but myself, and I decided that I was worthwhile. It no longer mattered that I would never get from mother or grandmother the love and acceptance I craved. It didn't matter who I was, what I did or what I owned, it was enough that I AM. I don't need to explain or to justify my existence. One of the most sacred names for the divine is I AM. Now I recognise that I share in the divine. I have always treasured the commandments, 'Thou shalt love the Lord (sic) thy God with all thy heart and with all thy soul and with all thy might. And thou shalt love thy neighbour as thyself.' To me, worship is recognising and communing with the divine, whether it is within myself, in others, or in the world. The pre-condition of worship is my belief in worth-ship, my own and that of other people.

I am more fortunate than many victims of incest; I can share this experience with you because I no longer feel any guilt or shame. De-privatising and re-cognising our experiences is important in finding our divinity. I also know that I have scarcely begun to understand the effect on my sexuality of being molested. But half an apple is better than none. I know I will have other opportunities to taste of the fruit of the tree and to become, as the wise serpent said, 'like gods, knowing good and evil'.

# Losing my Virginity

Consider rape.
I let him in my college room.
'Sure, you can sleep on my floor.'
It seemed daring but
I thought he was my friend.
Suddenly in the dark he spoke.
'Just let me in.'
What in my bed?
'Oh no I don't think I . . .'
Too late. He meant in *me*, anyway.
It hurt a lot.
I bled and bled and bled and bled.
When he felt the / saw the blood he went.
Leaving me to cope with the mess,
With myself.

# Eyes that Do Not See; Ears that Do Not Hear

Oppression in the extreme appears terrible, but oppression in more refined appearances remains oppression and where the smallest degree of it is cherished it grows stronger and more extensive. To labour for a perfect redemption from this spirit of oppression is the great business of the whole family of Jesus Christ in this world.

*John Woolman, 1720-72*

Until 1829 it was perfectly legal for husbands to beat their wives. The notion that women should be kept in order by their husbands did not die out when the law changed. Over 40 years later Frances Powers Cobbe's research[36] into the judicial records showed an astonishingly high incidence of wife chatisement. It was estimated that 6,000 women had been brutally assaulted over a three year period; this refers only to cases reaching the courts. Though many of the attacks were brutal the husbands were treated leniently. Not untypical was, 'George Ralph Smith, oilman, cut his wife . . . to pieces with a hatchet. He was found Not Guilty, as it was not certain that her death resulted from the wounds.'[37] Increased public concern about violence in marriage and in domestic service did result in some changes in the law. What, however, is the situation today?

Statistics are not easy to come by. Research occurs when the questions are being asked and it is only recently that the phenomenon of the battered wife* has been recognised. One study[38] looked at all the non-sexual offences involving violence dealt with by the police in Edinburgh and one district of Glasgow during 1974. Of the 3,020 violent incidents in these cities, over one-third were cases of family violence; three-quarters of these (1 in 4 of the total numbers of incidents) were cases of wife abuse. There is much concern, rightly, about child abuse; yet this accounted for only 1 in 25 of the incidents. Other studies[39] bear out these relative proportions.

Why is such a high incidence of violent acts against women in the home ignored? The situation is more serious when one takes into consideration the factors contributing to under-reporting: the shame at revealing family problems to public view; society's strongly held belief in the non-interference in family privacy; the lack of protection for women reporting such violence, yet having to live under the same roof as their attacker. The very term 'domestic violence' is misleading. It conceals the fact that it is overwhelmingly one sex that is the aggressor, the other the victim. Contrary to expectations, the women come from all social classes, so it is insufficient to lay the blame solely on the stresses of poverty. Nor is the battering an occasional phenomenon when the man is drunk, but is frequently systematic. The incidence of battering, as the statistics show, is higher than most of us imagine, too high to be dismissed as the actions of a few psychologically disturbed men. There is also a consistent pattern of guilt in the women. Though they are the victims they feel guilty that their marriage has failed and feel that they are the ones at fault.

Since 1981 I have worked with a Women's Aid Group. It has become more clear to me that the extreme violence experienced by women seeking refuge cannot be isolated from the attitudes of society, nor can I distance myself from them.

* The word 'wife' as used in this article refers to women living in relationships with men, whether married or not.

Violence towards wives often centres around the wife not fulfilling a perceived role. She must keep the house and look after the children, have meals ready on time, and generally see to the husband's comfort, all largely single-handed. She must account for her movements but must not question her husband's movements. She must be attractive to other men but in no way encourage them so that the husband's malehood is enhanced but not threatened. In cold print this sounds extreme, unreal, yet it is the reality for a great many women. To a greater or lesser degree we are all affected.

Incest is another area of abuse, where there is the same kind of under-reporting. Where rape crisis and incest survivors' groups have started, women immediately come forward to talk about their experiences for the first time and so start the healing process. One study has estimated that 25% of all females have had some kind of incestuous experience.[40] Even the more conservative figure of one in ten is still very disturbing.

The law responds unequally to the different types of indecent assault. Currently, though revision is underway, the maximum sentence for a sexual offence other than rape is 10 years if the victim is male, five years if the victim is a female under 13 years of age, and only two years if the victim is a female 13 or over. This highlights the way that, where the victim is female rather than male, our legislators (overwhelmingly male) perceive the situation with far less gravity.

We can acknowledge that women do get battered, raped and are incest victims; that there are less extreme violences in the form of sexual harassment; that structural violence is revealed in such facts as women's average earnings being only two-thirds those of men; whilst a cursory glance at the newsreels shows a conspicuous absence of women from the corridors of power, despite the notable exceptions. All this can be acknowledged and still many women will claim that they personally are not oppressed. Comparing oneself favourably in the context of the worst and most visible signs of injustice to women does not negate that injustice, nor put one outside it. Denying cherishes the oppression.

Having acknowledged the situation how can we respond? Perhaps the first step is to stop diminishing the problem and to accept the sheer depth and all pervasiveness of the injustice of women's place in society and the attitudes that sustain it. It then stops being 'the problem that has no name'. Then it is necessary to feel angry in the sense of being deter- mined to work for change. Quakers in particular often shy away from anger because they fail to make the distinction between two kinds, one destructive, the other empowering. That which is basically destructive, sees situations as not only wrong but hopeless. It sets out to destroy those seen as 'the enemy', the perpetrators of the wrong, asserting that no change is possible with the other still in existence. Energy is dissipated in outward violence or the inward violence of apathy. Empowering anger is creative. Though it points to injustices, brings about confrontation, this is healthy agita- tion based on respect for oneself and the other. It recognises that one side must change because it has been playing the part of a slave, and the other because it has been playing the part of a tyrant. Such anger is energising and can lead to creative action.

Such naming of the problem, such being angry, has led in the Women's Aid movement to positive action. Opening a refuge gives a safe place for a battered woman to go. From this direct practical action there has been a widening of the goals, of the vision. It is not enough to provide a safe place; one has to work to try and prevent the violence by increasing aware- ness of how and why it happens. Through consciousness- raising, as a result of women meeting and sharing their experience, comes the energy to work together for change.

The first Refuge opened in 1971. By 1975 there was a Com- mons Select Committee looking at violence in the family, actually recognising that a problem existed. We now have a Matrimonial Homes Act that improves women's right to the communal home; a Homeless Persons Act that allows women to be seen as homeless and to receive financial help if they leave a violent relationship; and new incest laws are being shaped. Much pressure from women's groups refusing to let the problems be ignored lies behind such new legislation. Prior to 1971, the battered wife was an unrecognised phenomenon and so could be largely ignored by professional groups. Since naming the problem, such professional groups are having to confront their reluctance to interfere in the family and to question received ideas about family dynamics.

As Quakers we pride ourselves on the place the Society of Friends has accorded to women over the centuries. If we truly have a vision of the uniqueness of each person that transcends gender as well as race, class and creed, where is our witness in the world? We have been clear in our Peace Testimony and have witnessed to it in the world often at great cost. Where is our witness against the injustice towards women?

# Such Stuff as Dreams are Made on . . .?

About five years ago I joined a small group of women to demonstrate against pornography outside the town's three sex shops. At that time I was not very clear in my own mind as to my *precise* objections to pornography; my exposure to it was limited to the *Penthouse* and *Mayfair* variety bought by my male peers at university. My reaction then was purely an intuitive one that somehow I felt personally implicated by these images of women, and that these images were selling lies about the nature of women's and men's sexuality. Further they were not simply inaccurate, but the stories they told were both degrading to me as a woman and sinister.

Some of the women carried placards, 'Porn is the theory: rape is the practice', 'Women say no to pornography', 'Pornography degrades women'. I was not prepared for what followed. Men passing by either laughed dismissively or became angry and abusive. 'It's always the ugly cows who object.' 'What you need is a good fuck.' One group crossed the street to us and made a point of going into the shop, where previously they had shown no interest in doing so. Coming out they thrust the centrefolds in our faces and jeered, 'What's wrong with this then?' Angry insults were thrown back and forth. Some of us approached men both inside and outside the shops, asking them to listen to our view that pornography was demeaning and degrading to women. One or two men even discussed the issues briefly.

One insisted, 'But I *love* women. What's wrong in enjoying physical beauty? This isn't degrading. Besides if you don't like it, don't buy it.' I wasn't very articulate in my arguments then. I didn't have an answer to the criticism that we were simply being 'prudes' and we had no right to impose our views on others.

Five years on I'm in a better position to argue my objections. I've made a point of looking at pornography and reading its stories. I've discussed the issues with men and women I know and I've read the arguments on both sides. Recently the development of my thinking has been massively accelerated by two major feminist texts: *Pornography and Silence* by Susan Griffin, and *Pornography: Men Possessing Women* by Andrea Dworkin. Having ploughed my way through Dworkin's book and the dreadful revelations it contains I cried and cried, for I shared something of Dworkin's misery at having discovered the tools for deciphering pornography's meanings, and then not wanting to know those awful truths. In the closing lines of her book Dworkin writes:

'I had been a hopeful radical. Now I am not. Pornography has infected me. Once I was a child and I dreamed of freedom. Now I am an adult and I see what my dreams have come to – pornography . . . In facing the nightmare I want another generation of women to be able to claim the dreams of freedom that pornography has taken from me.'

I too am infected by pornography. I cannot lose the knowledge I have gained, and my sexuality has been spoiled by that knowledge. Unlike Dworkin I have not lost all of my dreams; I believe in the possibility of change and I insist on it. For me it is vital to take some positive steps in face of the nightmare pornography has painted, and one such step is, I believe, to confront men and women with the existence of pornography, to ask that they consider and examine it, that they read and discuss feminist analyses of pornography and that if they reject those arguments they do so on stronger grounds than those of defensiveness.

It is not enough to dismiss pornography as a 'fringe issue' and 'nothing to do with me'. Neither you nor I can remain unaffected, for it is a pornographic culture in which we live.

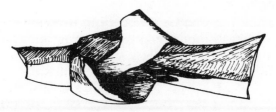

*Towards a definition of pornography*
It is a commonly held belief that 'pornography' refers to 'explicit sexual imagery intended to give erotic stimulation'. Accepting such a definition at face value, it would be hard to see what feminists could object to in this. Often debates about pornography and censorship focus narrowly on the rights of the individual to gain access to the pornography he desires. It follows then that the feminist anti-porn lobby is seen not only as prudish, but as attempting to set back the cause of liberty and freedom: to impose their neuroses on others, an outcome to be avoided at all costs by any intelligent person concerned with human rights and freedoms. Dworkin, tracing the historical roots of the word 'pornography' suggests a more accurate definition is, 'the graphic depiction of women as vile whores'. It is important to realise then, that feminist objections to pornography are not prudish objections to depictions of the erotic but to the very limited and damaging portrayal of woman whose identity and purpose is defined by her sexual function.

Whatever arguments are promoted by the defenders of pornography, the social message is the same: woman is object. Pornography is only and exclusively concerned with woman as material body: sensation without feeling. 'The pornographic camera performs a miracle in reverse. Looking on a living being, a person with a soul, it produces an image of a thing.'[41] This in itself is degrading and does violence to women's views of themselves.

## *Pornography: The Sado-Masochistic Ritual*

'If all the literature of pornography were to be represented by one performance, and if that performance were to move to its most dramatic moments, these would have to be the moments in which a woman is abducted by force, verbally abused, beaten, bound hand and foot, gagged, tortured, her body suspended wounded, then murdered.'[42]

Central to this ritual is the idea that physical and emotional release can be found through inflicting psychological pain on another. The form of sado-masochism may be milder or stronger, but the theme can be found in all shades of the market.

One might consider it an act of cruelty and degradation enough, to base a multi-million pound industry on a product promoting fantasies of woman as object, humiliated and damaged, but the cruelty goes one stage further. The porno-graphic message tells that women, far from suffering from men's sadistic treatment, perfectly complement the male style since they are inherently masochistic, deriving pro-found emotional and sexual satisfaction from being abused, coerced and brutalised. The implication of such a proposi-tion, that women can never really say no to sexual advances, that women need and relish force, violence and abuse to experience sexual pleasure is both obvious and sinister. In a society where male sexual domination exists both in reality and ideology, the perception of women as fickle whores provides a convenient rationalisation for men's treatment of them. As Dworkin comments, 'One does not violate something by using it for what it is: neither rape nor prostitution is an abuse of the female because in both the female is fulfilling her natural function'[43].

To me it is singularly clear that pornography cannot be considered as harmless fantasy of a neutral nature, nor can it be considered as a fringe interest outside existing power relationships between men and women. Pornography offers us many insights into aspects of men's assumption and use of power in our society, because it reflects the exercise of those powers in an undiluted and brutal manner. Men's power is backed up in our society by their almost universal occupation of key positions in society, their ability to articulate boundaries and define experience, their economic superiority and ownership, and above all their greater physical strength which enables them to exercise dominion over women.

*Pornography's educative role*

I think it very important for us to consider some possible effects of boys' and men's consumption of pornography on both the social construction of male sexuality, and on their attitudes and behaviour towards women.

I have recently started teaching in a comprehensive school and my 'specialty' is lower bands and remedial classes. Although I teach a number of different subject areas, the two subjects of most relevance here are 'Social Education' and 'Parentcraft'. Though 'Parentcraft' is mostly concerned with pregnancy and parenting, it does include some attempt to address the issues of inter-personal and sexual relationships. As far as it goes, all well and good. There are, however, two groups of pupils conspicuous by their absence – academically able pupils, and boys. There seems to be a hidden curriculum in those time-tabling arrangements. Firstly, that the area of inter-personal and sexual relationships is not a 'real' or 'legitimate' area of the curriculum and secondly, that this area of life is not relevant to boys. Although it is theoretically against the law to prevent either sex from studying particular options in state schools, the options are presented in such a way that would make it socially ostracising for any one boy to opt for this subject.

I have been given the opportunity to design my own course for the 'Social Education' class. (Anything as long as you keep them *in* the class room and fairly quiet.) Now approaching the topic of inter-personal relationships and sexuality with lively and sometimes disturbed fifteen year olds is hardly calculated to keep them quiet, but it has always kept them in the classroom where 'job application forms' has sometimes failed.

In approaching such topics two messages have come across loud and clear to me, their teacher. Firstly, that the girls in the group have developed more social maturity in the area of emotional relationships, and have far more information about contraception and sex matters. Secondly, that underneath a blustering exterior of bravado and worldliness the boys exhibit astonishing degrees of ignorance about sex, and an undisguised hostility towards the girls in the group – particularly those who are rumoured to have 'done it'. With one exception, these fifteen year olds (who will be joining adult society via the dole queue this year) have not received any information, or had any discussion with their parents about sex. Further, until now, any discussion they have had in school in this area has been narrowly restricted to the biology of reproduction.

In the absence of any positive education about how we choose friends, lovers, or partners, and what intimacy and sexuality is about, where do boys get their ideas? It is my feeling and my experience that they look (somewhat secretly and guiltily) to pornography, searching for some clue as to how to be sexual creatures or, in their terms how to be 'a man'. And what do they learn? That there are 'good women' and 'sexual women'; that a sexually attractive woman conforms to pornography's narrowly defined criteria, and that all women yearn to be ravished by a masterful man wielding a huge and relentless penis. (Note the stress involved in such a solo performance.) They learn also that sex is isolated from any other aspect of human social life, and that it is something a man does to a woman. No mention here of affection, exchange, reciprocity or intimacy.

If I am right, then we need to be very concerned about the misinformation pornography sells to boys and men in the gaps left by our half-hearted attempts to address 'sex education' in schools.

*Pornography: Image and Event*
　'There was a child went forth every day
　And the first object he looked upon, that image he became.
　And that object became part of him for the day, or a certain
　part of the day.
　Or for many years, or stretching cycles of years.'
　　　　　　　　　　　　　　*Walt Whitman 1819-92*

Behaviour, character and attitudes can all be shaped by the power of imagery, and pornographic imagery surrounds us wherever we go. Quakers can no longer hide their heads in the sand and deny its existence, or claim to be unaffected by it. We need to consider ways in which our own sexuality has been shaped by pornographic imagery, and to make the link between pornography, education and other aspects of women's subordination.

I am not suggesting that the censorship of pornography will provide the answer to all problems concerning male-female subordination. I recognise the difficulties in setting out guidelines for assessing what type of material is to be deemed offensive. What I am asking for is a willingness on the part of all those concerned with oppression and human liberation to make a serious personal examination of the content of pornography's messages about women, and to consider fully the arguments developed by feminists in response to those messages.

# A Parody of a Woman

I'm not an Amazon,
A bitch,
A cow or a cunt,
A drudge or an effing floosie,
A grannie or a hag (a right old bag),
Or even an indignant judie.

I'm not a Kali or a Kama,
A loose hot mama,
Or a no-good good-time girlie,
I'm not the other woman,
A prick-tease with a quim,
A mistress or a queenly mum.

I'm not a raunchy lady,
Always at the ready,
A shrew, or a slut or a slag with a slit,
I'm not a titillating tramp or an outright tart,
On the game, on the make (d'you fancy a bit?).
I'm not undying love or a virgin pure,
A witch or a gold-hearted whore,
I'm not foxy or exotic
Or sizzlingly erotic . . .
I'm a woman, not more.

# Not a Parody of a Woman

I am angry and assertive,
Brave and sometimes caring,
Cautious but at times
I am unusually daring,
Yes I know I'm energetic,
Funny too, I even find
That generally I'm generous,
Honest, just and kind,
Intuitive, yet logical,
Loving, look-you-in-the-eye,
Moving onwards, nice and open,
Pretty quick and rarely shy,
Yes I'm strong and full of talent,
Umpteen things as you might guess,
I'm very wise, and beyond description . . .
I'm a woman, nothing less.

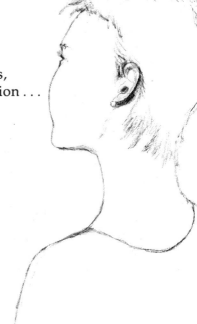

# Wars Begin in the Minds of Men

Since wars begin in the minds of men, it is in the minds of men that the defences of peace must be constructed.

*from the UNESCO Constitution*

When I first saw this quotation on a Quaker poster I was annoyed. The use of the term 'men' reinforces the supposition that war and peace are matters for male concern, too important to be entrusted to women.

On second thoughts, I agreed with the quotation. Most wars are planned and fought by men. But the quotation goes deeper than this. It challenges us to consider how we may detect the 'beginnings' of wars in the minds of men, and how we may construct the defences of peace. What are the beginnings of violence in the minds of men, and how do these manifest themselves in everyday life? Wars are not isolated phenomena; there are ways of leading up to them and away from them, behaviour which provokes them and which calms or stops them. They are part of the human process of relationships, on an individual, a national and an international scale.

How are the minds of men prepared for violence, so that they agree to participate in war? Military training exaggerates tendencies already introduced into men by a process of socialisation. The importance of football in building up team spirit, competitiveness, 'masculinity', etc., is at the heart of this socialisation process: 'The Battle of Waterloo was won on the playing fields of Eton.' Like Religious Education, football

is taught throughout the school system but, unlike R.E., it cannot be opted out of. Football teaches boys to subsume themselves into a team, to put the good of the team before their own good, to bear hurt if necessary for the glory of the team. This bearing hurt is important because, with fear of losing the esteem of one's team-mates, it reinforces the 'masculine' denial of feelings – makes them men. Then there is the competition, team against team, school against school. Without the 'them' there is no reason for the 'us'. This is the male bonding of the military, a rejection of 'femininity' and 'weakness'. That is, a process of depreciation of women. Violence against women is an integral part of making war: whether it manifests itself as verbal or physical abuse of women in the streets and homes of Britain; as a part of military training; or as acts committed during and after war, such as the humiliation, rape and murder of 'enemy' women. Such debasement of another human being arises from and reinforces the attitudes of mind in which war is seen as an acceptable or even a desirable activity.

Admittedly, even in the case of mass murder and rape, such acts are usually seen as being on a much smaller scale than acts of war. Is it not then over-dramatising to say that rape and wars spring from the same source? Increasingly, I find myself unable confidently to make the distinction, to say, 'Violence against women stops here, and wars begin here.' Rape has so often been a part of war and the language of war is used to describe 'masculine' sexuality: 'One man was discussing another man who seemed to be highly fertile – he had made several women pregnant. "That guy", he said, "doesn't shoot any blanks."'[44]

Violence is to do with power over others – whether physical, economic, intellectual or structural. Efforts to achieve power over others are common; within the military, personal status and international power are both highly prized. How can we expect men who, when they are seen to fail in some way, are taunted with names like 'girl' or 'faggot'; who are taught to equate 'success' with sexual and physical prowess and being a 'man' with the ability to hurt and kill – how can we expect these men to differentiate between violence against women and violence against countries? The one cannot exist without the other – at least, it seems never to have existed within the history of the military. The times when rape of enemy women is viewed as the prerogative of the victorious (or, indeed, any) army are still with us, and it is not only enemy women who are at risk. Even women serving in the armed forces are warned of the possibility of sexual attack by their male counterparts (who, after all, have been deliberately trained to believe that all things female are weak and worthless, with the possible exception of the Queen). Furthermore, both men and nations are rarely willing to accept blame or responsibility for their violent actions; we blame other countries for 'starting' wars just as men blame women for being raped (she was out on her own, hitchhiking, etc.).

It is a far cry, perhaps, from such men as these to that proportion of men who are not themselves physically violent. However, it is useful to examine war and violence against women as part of the same process, in order to gain an understanding of what is involved in violent behaviour, and of how the defences of peace can be constructed. Violence cannot endure without institutional power, and peace cannot endure without universal justice, yet many pacifists seem to me to have a limited conception of power and justice. Quakers are among those who work for disarmament, the right sharing of world resources, and an end to international conflict. We work for justice in the Third World, in prisons, in schools. Yet the defences of peace so constructed are lacking. In the early 1980s women comprised over half the British population, but only two-fifths of university students. On average, women's earnings were two-thirds those of men; not surprisingly, about three times as many women as men were forced to rely on supplementary pensions from the State. These are just some examples of the form institutional power takes in our society. It is, in many ways, as demeaning and dangerous to women as physical violence, to which it directly exposes some women. A recent report in *The Guard-*

*ian* described a woman who was stabbed eleven times by her husband, yet felt unable to leave him. The structural violence of society in denying her economic independence, a feeling of self-worth, and the knowledge that other ways of living are possible for women, is as guilty of destroying her life as is her husband. Indeed, her husband is also a product of the society.

The power of men over women which has existed historically in our society has long been accepted as 'normal' behaviour and consequently is not often recognised or questioned, even in the Society of Friends. In my understanding of that of God within me, I find Quakerism and feminism to be interdependent; yet I have met with astonishment, hostility, amusement and bewilderment from other Friends. In order to gain my rightful place in our Society I have to struggle against these attitudes, for I am not being treated justly. And the Friend who does not do me justice does me violence; not violence in the sense of assault or rape, but spiritual/emotional violence nonetheless, which precludes a state of true peace between us. Friends often assume that women will provide Monthly Meeting teas/look after Children's Meeting/not feel excluded when referred to as 'mankind' or 'brethren'. These unquestioned assumptions spring from and reinforce the stereotypes we have been taught to accept, and preclude the construction in our minds of the defences of peace. It is not enough to say, 'We do not kill', 'We do not rape'. Violence can be physical or systemic. Friends' treatment of and assumptions about women, both within and outside the Society, might not result in bruises and bloodshed, but they are still violent. Until each Friend sees this and strives to overcome it in her or his own life, and her or his relations with other individuals, we must face the fact that acts of violence are being committed, and that wars begin in the minds of Quakers as well as of others.

# On Fear and the Bogeyman

I went, a few years ago, to the Women's International Summer Event at Glastonbury. It was a long camping weekend held at Worthy Farm, the place where the big annual CND festival takes place. For the duration of the holiday the site was kept as 'women only' and there were maybe 600 women and girls staying at the camp, not a man nor boy to be seen. This woman's space left me with a major insight: I realised something about my ever present fear of male violence. I walked through the fields and campsites alone one night. There were strange shapes in the darkness, unfamiliar noises, people I didn't know moving around, and I was suddenly taken aback by the realisation that I was not afraid. I was in a strange place, in complete darkness and *I was not afraid*. I knew that there would be no men hiding in the bushes waiting to leap out and attack me. I knew that the unfamiliar presences around me were woman-shapes making woman-conversations, woman-noises. I did not understand before that moment how afraid I had been when I walked down a public street in the dark, or in remote, yet public, places even in the daytime. There had always been this mythical male who was waiting to jump out and hurt me. I'd assimilated this fear into my subconscious and it only became conspicuous by its absence.

I was attacked many years ago. It happened one Saturday

afternoon in the foyer of the block of flats where I lived alone. I was waiting for the lift and the lights, which were on time switches, went out. Suddenly this man, whom I hadn't registered as being present, attempted to attack me sexually. Although I wasn't formally trained in self-defence, I was physically strong and had talked through the potential situation before with friends. So I fought back and made a lot of noise, frightening him off before I was physically hurt or abused. Needless to say the mental scars and fear are still there. Sometimes I find the whole experience strengthening because the 'worst' had happened and I'd coped with the practicalities, but sometimes it's just a reminder that it could happen again.

Last weekend I went walking and spent a night out in the hills alone. It wasn't the first time I'd been backpacking solo but it had been a while since the last trip. The scenery was beautiful; there was silence all around apart from the occasional pheasant or rabbit that I disturbed and I rejoiced in my aloneness. I found a place to camp among some trees and by a stream. Before I fell asleep, and at times in the night when I awoke, I listened to the animal noises, worried by them at first. As I lay there I began to identify the screeching of owls and the rustlings as small animals made their way through the bracken. At one point a deer came to investigate. It sounds idyllic and it was, or would have been, if I could have rid myself of the persistent nagging fear of having been followed as I walked to that place. The chances of meeting another walker, or a forest ranger or gamekeeper on those hills were extremely slim; the hills are normally empty of any human life. But the doubt was there and it grew. Solitude has that effect on my worst thoughts. As I was walking along I found myself looking behind and about me, searching for the man in the bushes, gearing myself up 'just in case'. As I lay in my sleeping bag I waited for his approaching footsteps. I am still unsure about what it was that was making me afraid:

encountering a man bigger, stronger and fitter than me who would rape me or murder me; or being unable to summon help however loud I screamed; or being left badly hurt, unable to move? Probably all these and more.

Male violence towards women is something we are taught, mostly through the media, to be afraid of, but in the case of many women, myself included, it is something we have also experienced for ourselves. We all identify very strongly with the horrific stories reported in the press and in doing so our fear is reinforced. 'It could happen to me.' I feel so angry towards the sensational reports which help to cement that fear in place in my mind, while at the same time I wish that every woman's story of male-violence could be publicised to show how widespread it is. I feel angry towards the individual men who are so violent. But mostly my rage is directed at the mythical man in the bushes who is waiting for *me*, the fact that I subconsciously, or consciously, spend so much time and energy fearing *him*; the man I can't leave behind when I go walking in the hills alone, even though I long for the solitude. I am unable to exorcise him from my mind but I shall continue to try. And secretly I dream that one day I, and all women, will be able to go about in *our* streets and *our* countryside with that sense of freedom I felt as I walked through the fields near Glastonbury.

# For my Grandchildren

*(Greenham Common, 11th December 1982)*

I left Toby and Hannah
On the wire today,
Smiling out over the wintry scene,
Behind them the machines of war . . .

Before I left I raised my candle.
They were still smiling out into the darkness.
It broke my heart to leave them there,
Toby and Hannah
Hanging on the wire.

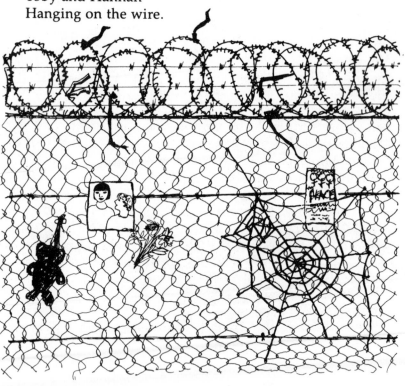

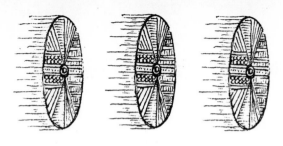

# Feminism, Greenham and Peace

In writing about peace and feminism I've come to realise that my knowledge of the two is in my guts and my heart far more than my head. For that reason I give you my personal story and experience. At first peace and feminism were two separate threads in my life. The first I was committed to, the other was a growing awareness. My story is of how the two became woven together until now I find I cannot see one without the other.

I've been involved in the peace movement since 1980 when I began to make the connections between nuclear power and nuclear weapons. I worked through many different areas: CND, Peace Tax Campaign, Quakers, local peace groups. I went on marches and rallies, attended conferences, spoke in public and wrote letters to papers and MPs. In December 1982 I joined the 30,000 other women who came to Greenham USAF base to surround the nine-mile fence. For me this was a turning point. It was the first time in my life I had been asked to do something that required only that I be a woman.

At Greenham the wheel of my life came unstuck and began to turn again. I was confronted by anger and pain in women proud to be women. I saw women openly and without shame weeping and mourning for those who had suffered and who continue to suffer as a result of the 'defence policies' of governments. I saw woman-loving women and I reeled under the impact of so much I had never dared to look at before.

I began to realise that for years I had bottled up my fear and anger. For years I hated it when I cried and hated myself for my emotional 'weakness'. I struggled to achieve a keen mind and to excel at argument and discussion. I tried hard and successfully to ignore my female body and to exist in my mind, desperately disassociating myself from the body that grew tired and hungry and let me down far too often. I took the weight of the world on my shoulders, never said no to any request to do work, never took time for myself and put myself last.

Slowly I reclaimed my body, saw how I had been mistreating and abusing it for years and took steps to get well again. As I nurtured myself back to health and no longer fought to keep my emotions at bay, I rediscovered tears and laughter and the capacity for joy. Women around me gave me amazing comfort and encouragement and I allowed myself to experience fully whatever emotion came up in me.

I came to realise that my personal journey was also part of a political process. I recognised our society as patriarchal, in the control of a male dominated ideology. I saw that my suffering, discomfort, pain and anxiety over the years were a result of my acceptance of those male values making me less than, and other than, my real womanly self.

Through all this period of personal change I continued to work within the peace movement and to be drawn back to Greenham again and again, like a bee to its hive.

At Halloween 1983 the women cut down the fence for the first time. Suddenly I saw the bases, the missiles, the fence, the 'Arms Race', the concept of the enemy, 'the other' as something belonging to the Patriarchy and particularly masculine. I knew as a result of reclaiming my body, my mind and my spirit as womanly that no woman could ever have invented that lot! I knew this in my deepest self, in a sense beyond words, and I wept and grieved over and over for what men have done to the world.

My weeping openly and my acceptance of my emotions I knew to be one key to the whole monstrous problem; learning to love my body and its rhythms and cycles another key. I discovered the power to act that came from opening out, sharing with other women, knowing them to be my sisters.

Looking around me with a new vision I saw that in the old view of the world emotions are taboo. Pain, grief, anger and fear are supposed to be hidden away. I had felt inferior because I was less able to control my emotions than the men around me. I was looked down on because I wept more, grew angry and impassioned over things, let my heart rule my head. I saw that the most successful men were those whose hearts were hardened and who were in total control of themselves. I tried to imagine Cruise missiles being deployed if those responsible allowed themselves to feel and imagine fully the terror, anguish and devastation that would result and knew that if they felt those emotions they could never bring themselves to be involved. I saw the same iron control of emotions being extended to men's physical powers; their superiority and supremacy over the natural world being exerted on every side. The desire to control and dominate is evident in the crazy way they live out their lives, risking cancer, heart disease, ulcers, total exhaustion. More evidence of the same desire is seen in the rat race, the space race, the conquering of the wilderness, of Everest, the breaking of the four minute mile, the sound barrier and the obsession with breaking record after record.

Men spend their lives in isolation from each other, their fear of other men dominating their existence. They turn to women for comfort and emotional support, women whom they see as softer, gentler, weaker and less threatening, and so they lose their ability to reach out to other men. Women are seen as a class apart, not as capable or as powerful as men, serving only as a support for men to make tolerable the intolerable world they have created.

But Greenham and the women's movement have meant that we women have been breaking out of our isolation, have seen reaching out to one another as a political act, as a way of reclaiming our joint power. Women are beginning to realise that together we are strong and can say 'no' to the whole terrible mess. We are not obliged to continue producing cannon fodder, we can demand a future for our children. We can cease to act as emotional props so that men can continue to destroy the earth. We need not be ashamed of the fact that we are female but can feel a new pride in shaking off the chains of the old world view and reaching out to the new.

More and more women both within and without the active peace movement are making the connections between the arms race and the Patriarchy. Men too are slowly beginning to see the connections for themselves. For me the hope for the future lies in the hands of women. Ian McEwan's oratorio asks, 'Shall there be womanly times or shall we die?' Frankie Armstrong, the feminist folk singer, replies, 'There will be womanly times; we will not die' and this I sing with her and with all my sisters from the bottom of my heart.

# Visitors at the Peace Camp

Daily I see them come,
bringing their gifts, their interest,
their obvious concern.
(I see some
off-load unwanted guilt
like the remains of picnic meals.)
I see them share our fire, our food
diffidently:
shield themselves
with admiration for our total commitment.
And I turn away sorrowful
from the projection of my own guilt
at being insufficiently committed.

# For the Policeman who Arrested me

I watched you as you stood in court
Reading from your xeroxed notes, your
Official evidence against me,
All about the court
The power of the law,
I watched you as you waited for a prompt
To speak, and then you said some more.
Your dark official uniform, its silver buttons,
Reflecting once again
The power of the law.
You must have been about my age,
Referring to your notes again, checking
What you saw
That day when you arrested me.
The words you read weren't real words,
Just jargon,
Just the power of the law.
And yet with all these legal trappings
You didn't really act so sure,
So certain of your evidence,
So certain of
The power of the law.
I watched you as I sang a song inside
Felt my strength grow, felt my spirits soar
And asked you for more details,
Questions, challenging, not you my friend,

But challenging and questioning
The power of the law.
You didn't try to cover up mistakes
In language that you'd made, nor
Did your gentle face set hard
Your eyes fixed on the courtroom floor,
My strength, my woman-power reaching you.
Yes, you were asking questions silently
Maybe questions that you'd never asked before
About the so called power,
The power of the law.
I liked that honesty in you
The human being that I saw
Behind that navy uniform,
Behind those buttons,
Behind the powerless,
Power of the law.

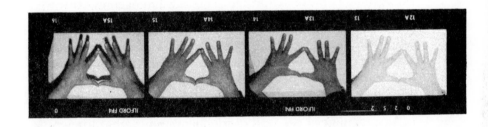

# What Canst Thou Say?

It is important to bring to mind our own experiences, to discover how we feel, why we feel it and to express it regardless of the oppression in our own heads – regardless of what others expect of us.

My view of life at forty is fundamentally different from what it was when I was a teenager. Then I accepted the stereotypes that women (and men) are brought up with. I was brought up to believe that complete fulfilment comes through marriage and motherhood. I believe now that we need to be more than someone's daughter, or someone's wife, or someone's mother; each of us needs to be a person in her own right. From my experience as a woman; as a daughter, a wife, a mother, I have been able to step forward and to grow spiritually.

As a teenager I was full of idealism about what life would be like. I married at twenty; now I see that as being signed over from my father to my husband. I gave up a career, quite ready (so I thought) simply to have a family. I began to learn what life was really like.

The reality of motherhood brought a dramatic change in my life: I lost my identity as a person in my own right. Through the nine months of carrying the growing baby inside me changes occurred in my body. Birth meant that suddenly I was completely responsible for another human being twenty-four hours a day, seven days a week. Although I had a good, loving and sharing husband, he did not feel the same sense of responsibility as I did. For my husband, wife and family were just additions to his life, to be taken into account along with his job and hobbies. He had a complete life outside the home. After the first blossom of fatherhood had worn off, he saw his contribution as that of being the provider.

The 'taking care of other', of husband and children, is mostly just taken for granted. The helpless new human being has to be fed, changed, loved and continually looked after. We become at the same time a nursery maid, a cook, a cleaner and a hostess. We do the washing and see there are clean clothes, we shop for food and cook it and always we must be aware of the requirements and feelings of others. Each day I started again: feeding, washing, shopping, cooking, cleaning, running errands, ready to chauffeur to and fro. Later I held down a part-time job as well. We are expected to teach a baby everything it must know to develop as a person in its own right, do all these jobs, be a wife, to the exclusion of ourselves.

The change in me began as the children got to their teens; they expected freedoms and experiences I had never had. Where was life going

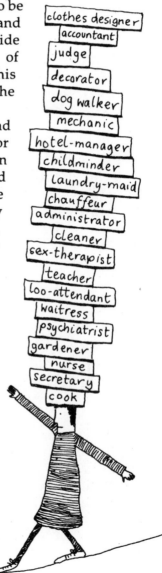

clothes designer
accountant
judge
decorator
dog walker
mechanic
hotel-manager
childminder
laundry-maid
chauffeur
administrator
cleaner
sex-therapist
teacher
loo-attendant
waitress
psychiatrist
gardener
nurse
secretary
cook

for me? What did I expect from it? I found I wanted the freedoms my children had; I wanted to travel, to meet new people and to learn to express myself.

The change in myself over recent years has been quite staggering. From finding I was not what I had expected myself to be, to finding what I really was – a competent person who still had potential for growth – was like being born again.

Many men and women are tied up in themselves, and in what others expect of them; they are not able, or are unwilling, to be free, to think and feel for themselves. By continuing to say and do what is expected of them they continue to feel safe and secure.

Having the confidence to go forward without the fear of 'what others will think' brings a new kind of security. The security of liking the person you are, of being in step with yourself. Before this stage is reached there is a great deal of work to do in learning to know yourself as you really are, through uncertainty, heart searching and prayer.

The effect of coming to realise what is inside of yourself and of facing up to it can be dramatic. If partners are not understanding or ready to listen, to stand back, wait, and help you through this change, then relationships and marriages can break down. Often one partner cannot understand or tolerate the different thinking, feeling and attitudes of the other. The person changing may feel a great deal of frustration, and so may their partner. Each does well to remember that these changes are not directed at the partner, family or Quaker Meeting. It may take a great deal of effort and searching to accept this. When the 'Door of Change' is opened, it is up to us as individuals whether we walk through it. We can only change our own attitudes, not those of others. We can only say to other people 'this is how I feel', 'this is what works for me', and hope that through our example, living our lives in the way we are sure is right for us, they will understand.

I had never been able to stand up in Meeting and express how I felt and wondered if I ever would. Other people could stand up and say what was inside 'Me', but I couldn't. At a Quaker residential weekend we were shown how to face up to our failings, to accept ourselves as we are, valuing our own gifts and individuality, and trusting in the spiritual Light Within as the first step to going forward. We were helped to learn how to use prayer to centre down to our inner being during worship in Meeting.

After this, one morning in Meeting I found words going round inside my head, linking my thoughts and feelings. I looked round everyone in Meeting wondering who would be the one to say it for me. Towards the end of Meeting I was quite shocked to find no-one had, and I was already standing up. What was I doing on my feet? What had I to say? Everything else was blank, so I spoke. This was an illuminating experience. From this beginning I have been able to experience a deep sense of spiritual worship and on occasion to share it.

As I have increasingly attended the Quaker Women's Group, it has been a great support to find so many others like myself who have had to learn for themselves and really step forward by themselves through a continual pain of misunderstanding, or of others just not wanting to know. I believe that our way must not be to set women against men, but for us women to show how we have learned to express ourselves. Men, if they so wish, have the opportunity to do the same. I believe that if we work by example, accepting ourselves, through the Light Within, then spiritual growth will follow.

clothes designer

Judge

laundry-maid

childminder

chauffeur

administrator

87

cleaner

# Destiny

A caterpillar at its death
may become an oak-tree
or a butterfly.
Either way it must enter the chrysalis
of its own choosing alone
and endure the patient waiting
that acts upon it for eternal change.

In this fluid state
of not-being anything
capable of independent action,
I have chosen to not-be butterfly.
Instead I will become a giant oak
and change the course of history
and evolution.

# ... A Gift of God

Having been brought up in a Quaker family, I felt that while I accepted generally the social and 'political' implications of Quakerism, I lacked experience of the spiritual aspects; somehow the idea of God, Jesus, and religion generally didn't ring true for me. My understanding was on a theoretical level, not based on personal experience. Consequently I did not feel any desire to continue going to Meeting when I left home to go to university, and I attended only occasionally during the holidays, primarily in order to see people I liked and respected.

After university, I was able to go to work with the Quaker U.N. Office in New York for a year. An interest in the spiritual aspects of Quakerism revived in me partly, I think, because of the need to find something deeper and more restful than the bustle of the U.N. and the clamour of New York. I went to Meeting often, and found there an opportunity to reappraise my ideas of God in general and religion in particular; things began to make more sense as I began to appreciate what God could mean to me. I became very involved in the life of the Meeting, made some wonderful friends, attended worship-sharing sessions, and a Bible-study group, and generally grew to delight in the wealth of personality and spiritual insights of the people around me.

By this time I felt very strongly that Christianity, if not entirely dependent upon the subordination of women by men, at least perpetuated the discrimination which existed in society. Our Bible-study group was interrupted frequently by my indignation at the degree of negation and oppression of women that I found in the gospels we read, and I felt more and more convinced that Christianity did not speak to me as a woman, and did not answer my spiritual needs. However, I did find myself becoming more and more attracted to Quakerism. Admittedly, New York's 15th Street Meeting is not typical of Meetings either in Britain or in the States. Its members and attenders come from a breath-taking range of backgrounds and life-styles, each making their own distinctive contribution to the Meeting. It was here that I had the space to discuss a feminist approach to Quakerism with women from the Women's Meeting; to understand that a Christ-centred approach to Quakerism was not part of the experience of the many New York Friends from Jewish backgrounds; to listen to the Friend who was familiar with the life and beliefs of Eastern mystics. All these Friends expressed their conception of 'that of God within' in terms which, for the first time, I instantly understood and responded to. On one occasion, during a discussion in the Bible-study group, one Friend suggested that oneness with God could not be achieved without complete self-knowledge and identity. This thought has stayed with me ever since – somehow it seemed to make complete sense. I formally began the Search to Find Myself!

This is an exciting and stimulating, but rather long-winded process. An integral part of it is my feminism – at the same time that I 're-discovered' Quakerism, I was attempting also to live as a feminist, putting feminist ideals into practice, and somehow the two seemed to merge naturally together. All this time I continued to experience the facilitating and mediating role of Quakers at the U.N., I continued to participate in the peace vigil each Saturday on Fifth Avenue, and I continued to feel that all these different aspects of my life were inextricably bound up in each other. I was a pacifist, a feminist, and a Quaker: I was – and still am – completely unable to separate any of these strands of my being. When I returned to Britain I joined the Quaker Women's Group, which I have found to provide exactly the sort of Quaker feminist support and spirituality which I need.

After my return from New York, the idea that I might be homosexual periodically suggested itself to me. These periods of questioning became more insistent until, at a Quaker Women's Group weekend gathering on the theme of 'sexuality', I mentioned my thoughts to some of the women there. They were very supportive and I left the weekend feeling that I had a lot to think about and work through, but also feeling very optimistic. One of the women lent me her copy of *Meeting Gay Friends*[45] discreetly wrapped in brown paper! Before I began to read it, I had tried an experiment which was to say to myself 'I am a Lesbian', just to see what it felt like. It felt wonderful! I was *very* surprised. Suddenly, everything seemed to fall into place. Hundreds of past events came into focus and I understood them as I had not done before. I felt secure and self-confident. Surely something must be wrong? I had expected to go through mental agonies and anguish before being able to accept being gay, but it didn't happen. Then one, in particular, of the accounts in *Meeting Gay Friends* hit me right between the eyes – someone else had felt like I did!

The following weekend I spent with my parents. As my feeling of euphoria wore off slightly I realised that my relationship with them was such that I could, and had to, tell them. I had been afraid that, even subconsciously, such news might make them feel differently about me, but they couldn't have responded to me in a better way. For this, and for the support of friends in the Quaker Women's Group, I will always be grateful.

Recognition (and welcome) of my sexuality helped me see

91

myself a lot more clearly – I felt I had overcome an immense hurdle on my path of self-knowledge, and I do feel a certain sense of 'oneness', of unity, which convinces me that I am going in the right direction. It is often said that God moves in a mysterious way, although I believe that Friends will feel that to develop someone's spirituality through Lesbian feminism is one of God's rather more mysterious movements. It is partly for this reason that I feel I must turn to the Quaker Women's Group (and possibly to the Friends Homosexual Fellowship) for support and spiritual growth, as well as to Meeting for Worship. Whatever happens, and whatever difficulties the future may hold, I will always be grateful for the feeling of enlightenment which has marked this particular stage of my spiritual journey. It is for this reason that I view my homosexuality as a gift from God.

# Faith

In the movement between the worlds
Faith is born
Like sunlight she dances among the shadows
(A falling leaf plays a melody
And a tree smiles)

In the movement between the worlds
Faith is born
Born between hands gently holding companionship
Moving through time without haste
In joyfulness

In the movement between the worlds
Faith is born
In the depths of the eyes of infinite knowings
She sees herself reflected
And hears her name

In the movement between the worlds
Faith is born
In fountain bursts of longing she cries out—YES!
Returning silence resonates
She breathes,
'Here I Am'

# We Do Earnestly Desire and Wait

*that by the Word of God's power, and its effectual operation in the hearts of men, the kingdoms of this world may become the kingdoms of the Lord . . .*[46]

Waiting, watching, witnessing, women looking on from a distance – Mary Magdalene, Joanna, Salome, Mary the mother of James and Joseph, the mother of Zebedee's children, many other women who came up with Jesus unto Jerusalem – present at his crucifixion, sitting over against the sepulchre watching at his burial, first witnesses to his resurrection. Women walking to the tomb at first light, hands full of sweet spices, knowing for a fact that they did not have the physical strength to move the stone aside. 'And they said among themselves, who shall roll us away the stone from the door of the sepulchre?'[47] It didn't stop them, the knowing they could not get in, the fact that what they proposed to do was impossible. They went anyway, 'and when they looked, they saw that the stone was rolled away'[48].

Waiting, watching, witnessing, women at the Greenham fence, present as the death of the planet is rehearsed by men acting in our name, the death of thousands of unknown women who live at a distance, in a country where men practise our death. I stood at the fence one night in September, feet rooted to the muddy ground, hands deep in my pockets, watching through the wire that flat ravaged land that is now never dark, never quiet, imagining through the fence a field of bracken and scrub, a field of flowers, a field of corn, a field of children playing. Red police car, blue lights flashing, 'What are you doing, then, love? Not cutting the fence are you?' 'No, just praying at it.' A soldier with a dog walks up and down inside, suspicious, watching me watching him. 'Good evening.' 'Good evening.' I wait, not knowing what I'm waiting for. The kingdoms of the Lord? A hundred yards to my left, women cut the wire, roll away the stone, and walk through into the tomb. No angels greet them; no resurrection yet.

Yet still women witness to that possibility, the possibility that something may be accomplished which in our own strength we cannot do. Women waiting, watching, just being there, behaving as if peace were possible, living our dream of the future now. 'Why do you come here? Why do you keep coming?' – a soldier near Emerald camp on an earlier visit – 'It's no use, there's nothing you can do, what do you women think you can do by coming here? The missiles are here, you won't change anything, why do you come?' We come to watch, we come to witness, we come with our hands full of ribbon and wool, flowers and photos of loved ones, hands full of poems and statements and prayers, hands full of hope and the knowledge that such hope is impossible to rational minds. I come to be with the women who live here, the dykes, the dropouts, the mothers and grandmothers, angels with countenances like lightning. I come to talk with the police, the soldiers, men who might be gardeners standing by the tomb; I come to meet the Christ in them.

It doesn't just happen at Greenham, of course – though that is where I first consciously felt it, the positive force of this waiting, and began to give it a name. It happens everywhere, every day, women in impossible conditions, in impossible relationships, living as if those relationships, those conditions were possible. Hand in hand, ordinary women declaring, 'We know there is a healthy, sensible, loving way to live and we intend to live that way.'[49] Nurses, midwives, teachers, lovers, nurturers, healers, prophets, witnessing over and over in our common lives to the transforming power of love, the power of our anger and determination on behalf of those we love. Again and again I have walked to the tomb of a friendship, a working relationship, a love affair, with sweet spices in my hand, refusing to accept that there was no way I would be able to get in. We know, we women, we know all about earnestly desiring and waiting, about loving and suffering and going on anyway, witnesses to a different reality, a different way, an impossible possibility of resurrection.

And we have always known, although the importance of that knowing has been hidden from us. It didn't seem significant, somehow, to the men who wrote the gospels, the men who write the history books. They glossed over it. They continue to gloss over us, sitting over against the sepulchre, looking on from a distance, women without faces, without names – 'the wife', 'Greenham woman', 'love', 'Zebedee's kids' mum'. But we've been there, all the same; we are still here, witnessing, watching. 'Therefore wait, for the Lord is doing great things for this darkness, and this heathenish ministry and dark power hath long reigned.'[50]

Now, once again, it is time. Women of our generation crowd forward, voices rich with the sound of rushing wind, wills bright as tongues of flame. From our mothers, for our children, we reclaim the importance of our knowing, the power of our waiting. Hands full of sweet spices, we walk once again to the tomb. It won't take much. Just the rolling away of a stone. Just a different way of seeing things that have always been, a different way of knowing truths we have known all along

> . . . *that thereby all people, out of every profession, may be brought into love and unity with God, and one with another, and that they may all come to witness the prophet's words, who said 'Nation shall not lift up sword against nation, neither shall they learn war any more.'*[51]

97

# References

## Interweaving Quakerism and Feminism, pp. 1–8

[1] Olive Schreiner quoted in *Christian Faith and Practice in the Experience of the Society of Friends*. London Yearly Meeting of the Religious Society of Friends, 1960, §257 (hereafter referred to as *CF&P*)

[2] *The Journal of George Fox* ed. John Nickalls. Cambridge Univ. Press, 1952, reptd. London Yearly Meeting, 1975, p. 11, quoted in *CF&P*, §5

[3] From 'The testimony of Margaret Fox concerning her late husband' quoted in *CF&P*, §20

[4] From 'Report of the International Council of Women' (1888) quoted in *Significant Sisters* by Margaret Forster. Secker & Warburg, 1984, p. 233

[5] George Fox, Epistle 275 (1669) quoted in *CF&P*, §280

[6] From the Preface to *Daughters of Copper Woman* by Anne Cameron. The Woman's Press, 1984

[7] George Fox, Epistle 10 (1652) quoted in *CF&P*, §406

## Bringing the Invisible into the Light, pp. 9–10

[8] Lucretia Mott from a speech she gave in 1852 to a Woman's Rights Meeting, West Chester, Pennsylvania, USA. Quoted in *Lucretia Mott Speaking: excerpts from the sermons and speeches of a famous nineteenth century Quaker minister and reformer*. Pendle Hill Pamphlet 234, 1980, p. 14

## Women and the Society of Friends, pp. 11–20

[9] T. S. Eliot 'Burnt Norton' in *Four Quartets*. Faber, 1944, p. 7

[10] George Fox, *Journal*, op. cit., p. 96

[11] *Ibid*, p. 8

[12] From 'The Women's Yearly Meeting' by Mary Jane Godlee in *London Yearly Meeting during 250 years*. Society of Friends, 1919, p. 97

[13] George Fox, quoted in *The Beginnings of Quakerism* by William C. Braith-

waite. Second edn. rev. by Henry J. Cadbury. Cambridge Univ. Press, 1955, p. 341

[14] George Fox, *Journal*, op. cit., p. 667
[15] From 'Testimony to the life of Anne Whitehead' in *Piety Promoted*, 1686
[16] William Loddington, *The Good Order of Truth Justified* . . . London, 1685
[17] Minutes of London Yearly Meeting, 1766
[18] Rebecca Jones, quoted in *The Later Periods of Quakerism* by Rufus M. Jones. Macmillan, 1921, vol. 1, p. 116
[19] *Friends Quarterly Examiner*, 1894, p. 195
[20] Letter from John Southall quoted in *Journal of the Friends Historical Society*, vol. xvii, p. 85
[21] Ms. letter dated 3rd of Fourth Month, 1896 in Friends House Library, London
[22] Margaret Hope Bacon, *The Quaker Struggle for the Rights of women*. AFSC, 1974, p. 3
[23] *A Testimony for the Lord and his Truth, given forth by the Women Friends at their Yearly Meeting at York* . . . York, 1688

## Bad Language, pp. 23–27

[24] Casey Miller & Kate Swift, *Words and Women: New Language in New Times*. Anchor/Doubleday, 1976, pp. 25–6
[25] Alma Graham, *The Making of a Non-Sexist Dictionary*. Rowley, Mass., USA: Newberry House, 1975, p. 62
[26] From a paper *Paradigmatic Woman: the Prostitute* by Julia Stanley. Linguistic Society of America, 1973
[27] Dale Spender, *Man Made Language*. Routledge & Kegan Paul, 1980, p. 16
[28] Jenny Cheshire, 'A Question of Masculine Bias' in *English Today*, 1985, vol. 1, p. 24

## Gospel Truth, pp. 33–35

[29] Elaine Pagels, *The Gnostic Gospels*. Weidenfeld & Nicholson, 1980
[30] *Ibid*, p. 48
[31] Iranaeus, quoted in *Ibid*, p. 50
[32] *Ibid*, pp. 49–50
[33] *Ibid*, p. 51
[34] 'Gospel of Philip' 63:2–64:5 in *Nag Hammadi Library*. E. J. Brill, 1978, p. 138. Quoted in Elaine Pagels, *op. cit.*, p. 64
[35] 'Pistis Sophia' 36:71 quoted in Elaine Pagels, *op. cit.*, p. 65

## Eyes that Do Not See, Ears that Do Not Hear . . . pp. 53–57

[36] 'Wife torture in England' by Frances Power Cobbe in *The Contemporary Review*, April, 1878, p. 71

[37] *Ibid*, p. 74

[38] R. Emerson Dobash and Russel Dobash, *Violence against wives*. London: Open Books, 1979

[39] F. H. McClintock, *Crimes against the Person*. Manchester Statistical Society, 1963

[40] Judith Lewis Herman, *Father-Daughter Incest*. Harvard Univ. Press, 1981, referring to Kinsey and others, *Sexual Behaviour in the Human Female*. Saunders, 1953

## Such Stuff as Dreams are Made on . . .? pp. 58–65

[41] Susan Griffin, *Pornography and Silence*. The Women's Press, 1981, p. 36.

[42] *Ibid*, p. 46

[43] Andrea Dworkin, *Pornography: men possessing women*. The Women's Press, 1981, p. 203

## Wars Begin in the Minds of Men, pp. 68–72

[44] 'More power than we want: masculine sexuality and violence' by Bruce Kokopeli and George Lakey in *Reweaving the Web of Life* ed. by Pam McAllister. Philadelphia, USA: New Society Publishers, 1982, p. 233

## . . . A Gift of God, pp. 89–92

[45] *Meeting Gay Friends: essays* ed. by John Banks and Martina Weitsch. Friends Homosexual Fellowship, 1982

## We Do Earnestly Desire and Wait, pp. 94–97

[46] From 'A declaration from the harmless and innocent people of God, called Quakers . . .' in *Journal of George Fox*, op. cit., p. 400

[47] *Mark*, 16:3 (Authorised version)

[48] *Mark*, 16:4 (Authorised version)

[49] Women's Pentagon Action Unity Statement (a collectively written working statement, 1982) quoted in Pam McAllister, *op. cit.*, p. 415

[50] From a letter written by Margaret Fell to Francis Howgill and James Naylor when they were prisoners in 1653, excerpted in *Margaret Fell Speaking* by Hugh Barbour. Pendle Hill Pamphlet 206, 1976, p. 23

[51] From 'A declaration from the harmless and innocent people of God, called Quakers . . .', *op. cit.*

# Contributors

We are a group of white women and in this book we have spoken for ourselves but we hope our words may touch the lives of women everywhere. For every woman who actually wrote of her experience, there may be countless others who recognise it in their own. We have chosen not to link our names directly to the text; rather, we hope the reader will accept each piece as it stands. The following list of contributors includes the names of women who have, in any way, been involved in the process of bringing the book to fruition:

Anne Wilson ~ Barbara Millard ~ Celia Ashworth
Clare Yerbury ~ Doreen Osborne ~ Doreen Wilson
Elisabeth Seale Carnall ~ Eve Heelas ~ Evelyn Mudd
Gil Isaacson ~ Gil Skidmore ~ Heather Stent
Helen Armstrong ~ Helen Gould ~ Isobel McCallum Clark
Jackie Scully ~ Jane Heydecker ~ Jane Serraillier Grossfeld
Jennifer Barraclough ~ Jenny Cross ~ Jill Wilsher
Kim Chenoweth ~ Kim Puttick ~ Lindsey March ~ Lis Burch
Magda Cross ~ Marieke Clark ~ Mary Lou Leavitt
Mary Synott ~ Mary Frances ~ Mary Wakeling
Maureen Graham ~ Maureen Lofthouse ~ Morning Martin
Pam Brunt ~ Pat Hibbs ~ Patience O'Leary
Patricia Moot Craven ~ Phoebe Spence ~ Rita Calvert
Sara Leaf ~ Susan Rooke-Matthews ~ Teresa Smith
Una Parker (Ackworth) ~ Zoe White
– supported and prayerfully upheld by many others.